WHITE SUPREMACY
HISTORY

THE NEVER-ENDING FIGHT AGAINST RACISM

FOR THE ACHIEVEMENT OF CIVIL RIGHTS

George Parker

TABLE OF CONTENTS

INTRODUCTION

Laws sometimes don't change people's minds, even when they say we're all the same. They just serve as a watershed to history. The United States abolished slavery in 1865. And they slaughtered themselves to do it. The abolitionist North versus the slave South. A war of secession; four years of fighting, and cities destroyed, with innocent victims. But it didn't take a hundred years to say a black man was the same as a white man. On October 2, 1962, in the state of Mississippi, blacks could not attend white people's universities. To assert their rights, they had to face a segregationist uprising. The army intervened; there were clashes and deaths. President Kennedy spoke. But the road to equality was a long one. And it had to go through the murder of Martin Luther King, the birth of Black Power, the rise of Malcolm X. The sensational protest over the podium at the 1968 Mexico City Olympics with Smith and Carlos' black-gloved fist. Even today, despite the Affirmative Action, the blacks still clash with creeping racism that excludes them from the places of power. Barack Obama's election has stirred things up, but the tragic killings of African-American boys by law enforcement officers are proof that racism has not been defeated. In the southern states, the difference is palpable. In the megalopolises of the East Coast, there are still entire suburbs left to degradation and petty crime with a predominantly black population. All it takes is nothing but a spark to spread the fire of a revolt.

While this book is printing, there is an unprecedented protest in the United States across the globe. The demonstrations and riots are not understandable in all their reasons and implications except within the broader context of **the systematic oppression and discrimination of African Americans in the United States, and their historical origins**.

Although the Declaration of Independence of the United States notoriously states that "all men were created equal," the Founding Fathers thought of men with a skin of a precise color. The defense of slavery from the growing hostility of the English was indeed one of the reasons, and the one less willingly spoken of, in the United States, and for which Americans sought that same independence. Slaves were not considered human beings: their condition was hereditary and perennial, and individual slaves could be exchanged, dismembered, sold, mutilated, bought, raped, pledged, given as gifts. Nothing could belong to the slaves, not even their children; everything could be made of them, and everything was done to them. The few Afro-Americans who could redeem themselves from cages and chains, literally speaking, we're often killed with impunity; their enterprises were destroyed if they dared to open one, and their fortunes were plundered.

It was continued long after the formal abolition of slavery, which was after a war in which hundreds of thousands of people had died to defend it, through the legal imposition of real apartheid built to continue to treat blacks as subhumans and isolate them from public life. "Separate but equal," the Supreme Court ruled, but there was nothing equal. Informal segregation was omnipresent. Everything existed in two versions, from schools to phone booths, from parking lots to cemeteries, and only one of them was dignified; that was the violent subjugation of blacks, who could not testify against a white man and had to make room for him on the sidewalks or at the bar counter; who were subject to all kinds of bullying. No real emancipation could be allowed. After preventing blacks from learning to read and write for centuries, it was established that only those who knew how to do so could vote. When with the New Deal, the federal government pledged to support the real estate market through state-guaranteed mortgages, it decided that these benefits would not go everywhere: neighborhoods inhabited mostly by African-Americans were highlighted in red on maps, hence the name that took this practice, "redlining," and they would not perceive anything.

Still in the middle of the 20th century, successful African-American entrepreneurs were killed and robbed without consequences, while those who dared to rebel were lynched. Things have changed slowly and inexorably, fortunately, but they are still far from ordinary. The functioning of the judicial system over the years, for example, still reflects this asymmetry: there is not a single type of crime that does not yet see a large disproportion of penalties and sentences to the disadvantage of blacks; the progressive instrumental tightening of the rules has allowed even thirteen-year-old boys who had committed non-violent crimes to be sentenced to life imprisonment. They are almost all black people: as are the majority of those detained in the United States. This country puts proportionately more people in prison throughout the world, although African Americans make up 13% of the population. Meanwhile, stories of blacks killed by the police at a checkpoint or in the middle of the street are circulating weekly, with no consequences, and many states continue to seek rules and quibbles to limit the participation of African Americans in elections.

Flint, Michigan

In a nation that is only three hundred years old and has spent two hundred and fifty years subjugating blacks with the full force of the state, the Civil Rights Act only dates back to 1964 Such systematic segregation with such deep roots spontaneously reproduced itself in Flint when its economic system collapsed. Most whites got away with it or left, while most blacks stayed, and no one took care of the city anymore except to commission it and ignore almost two years of protests while people drank toxic waste. Deindustrialization hurt all of Michigan, but a few places hurt as much as Flint: while Flint sank and its children suffered irreparable damage, a few miles away, there was still some way to stay standing, in a city that had at least clean water and asphalt without potholes. As Richard Manning, a journalist and writer originally from Flint wrote, what happened was a kind of little social experiment: it's not that places like Flint were the only ones with problems in Michigan or the Midwest, but those are the places where the border was drawn. In places like Flint, a kind of externalization of difficulties has been practiced for decades, so everything that worked was progressively taken away, and everything that didn't work was abandoned there. Hence, another crisis followed every crisis. Every disaster was followed by another failure, giving the city as irrecoverable and, in this way, making it effectively irrecoverable.

George Floyd has now become the symbol of a protest rooted in history. With this book, we want to go through it, to immerse ourselves in events that have marked the soul of a people that still today continues to demand a ransom that has never arrived.

The souls have been shaken, and now a new page must be written so that those words spoken after the march on

Washington will never again be limited to a dream, but a reality:

> *I have a dream that one day this nation*
> *will rise up and live out the true meaning*
> *of its creed: "We hold these truths to be*
> *self-evident, that all men are created*
> *equal."*
>
> - M. L. King

CHAPTER 1 – THE ORIGINS

What's racism?

It is the vision of humanity divided into "superior" and "inferior" races based on biological inheritance. According to this theory, the development of the history of humanity would be a consequence of the predominance of superior races over inferior ones. The full debate began at the turn of the 19th and 20th centuries on the "question of race," and in particular on the social and political consequences of biological differences between human groups. However, at the end of this century, scholars agree that the real problem is not racial differences, but rather the negative meaning that racism, understood both as a doctrine and as a practice of discrimination, attributes to them.

The term "race," from which *racism* derives, is of uncertain origin and was introduced in European languages around the 16th century; it was used in the Book of Martyrs (1563) by John Fox to indicate the lineage: in this case the "race and strain of Abraham." From the 16th century onwards, to explain the differences between Africans, Chinese, and Europeans, instead of the term race, the genealogies of the different ethnic groups described in the Old Testament were used. When, at the end of the 17th century, the debate on the morality of the slave trade between the two sides of the Atlantic developed, those who were against slavery underlined the fact that blacks and whites shared common humanity. The term race returned to be used about the relative technological backwardness of Africans, which was considered the result of their unhealthy living conditions (due both to the climate and the lack of political and social institutions to promote their progress) and which were the basis of attempts to legitimize discrimination first, and slavery later. Not even Charles Darwin's book "The Origin of the Species" (1859), which documented how development was produced by natural selection and which revolutionized the theories on differences between human beings in the scientific field, could prevent a distorted use of the term race. He inspired, indeed, a new form of racism; the so-called "scientific racism," based on the idea that racial prejudice even performs an evolutionary function. The sociological theory of racism dates back to the early 1920s, when some psychologists began to argue, exhibiting extensive documentation, that racial prejudice was not a hereditary characteristic, but a form of behavior learned during socialization. Every society has its own culture and, at the same time, is subject to a series of cultural prejudices. Ethnocentrism is, in fact, the tendency to reason and make judgments "as if one's own culture and ethnic group were at the center of the world." Concerning skin color, individuals can, for example, share the preferences of the social group in which they are placed and therefore treat those who do not belong to it with mistrust.

Or, as in Japan, the majority can avoid contact with the Burakumin, an ethnic minority from a professional caste formed during the feudal period.

The caste system in India or apartheid in South Africa also represents forms of discrimination very similar to racial discrimination.

The biological theory

The biological theories about the race underwent profound changes in the 1930s. With the emergence of genetics, which documented how not the species but the gene, was the unit of selection, it was possible to speculate that there were potentially as many races as there were genes. But in 1939, Julian Huxley and Alfred Cort Haddon, in the book "We Europeans," argued that groups, usually considered races, were not biological phenomena, but political inventions, and that it would be correct to call them "ethnic groups."

Immigration as a cause of racism

Racism can also be a consequence of migratory phenomena. They are generally caused by economic reasons and, in particular, by the lack of job opportunities in the regions of origin. Migratory events, when they occur to areas of scarce resources and economic insecurity, are often perceived as a threat to the well-being of local populations. This gives rise to a feeling of general intolerance and distrust towards newcomers: the term used to describe this attitude is xenophobia (from the Greek "fear of the foreigner"). Although they may share some characteristics, xenophobia and racism are nevertheless different phenomena: while the former consists of a hostile attitude towards the foreigner perceived as a threat, racism conceives the immigrant as belonging to an inferior race.

The I.Q. as an excuse for racism

In the Sixties the spread of the practice of intelligence testing rekindled in the scientific world the controversy about the heredity of intelligence (or rather, of that particular concept of knowledge detected by intelligence quotient tests, I.Q.), giving new impetus to forms of racism based on the alleged inferiority of certain ethnic groups. Scientifically proving how behavior or characteristic is a product of heredity or a consequence of socialization is, however, complicated. Those who support the first hypothesis have, therefore, been accused of encouraging new scientific racism. The linguist William Labov has documented, thanks to numerous studies, how tests build intelligence rather than measure it. In one of his articles, Black Intelligence and Academic Ignorance (*Black Intelligence and Academic Ignorance*-1972), he argued that intelligence tests are ethnocentric because they are based on a narrow concept of intelligence, that of logical operations, typical of Western culture and where it is obvious that white people are on average more skilled, at least in the short term. The results of the test would, therefore, have nothing to do with genetic differences but would only reflect the ethnocentric way in which the test is formulated.

Slavery

Slavery is the condition of one person entirely and involuntarily subjected to another. The constitutive characteristics of slavery are:

- coercion to perform a task or service;
- the reduction of a human being to the exclusive property of another human being, that is, his master;
- the complete submission of an individual to the will of the one who possesses him.

The exploration of Africa, the invasion of the Americas by Europeans in the 15th century, and the subsequent colonization of these territories over the next three centuries gave a significant boost to the slave trade. Portugal, which needed agricultural workers, was the first European state to use slaves as early as 1444 to meet its domestic labor needs. By 1460 it was already importing between 700 and 800 slaves a year from the west coast of Africa. Spain soon followed the Portuguese example but failed, at least initially, to undermine the Portuguese monopoly of the African slave trade. In the same years, the trade in African slaves from Central Africa to the Arab, Iranian, and Indian markets were also intensified by Arab traders. A sharp increase in the demand for slave labor was a consequence of the harsh conditions that Spanish colonization imposed on the indigenous population in Latin America. The hard work in the fields, the poor hygienic conditions, and the diseases brought from Europe contributed to decimating the community, which was replaced by African slaves, believed to be better able to withstand arduous work, such as growing sugar cane in tropical climates. In North America, the first African slaves were settled in Jamestown, Virginia, in 1619. Initially, it was not considered necessary to proceed to a legal definition of their status, but from the second half of the 17th century, with the development of plantations in the colonies of the South, the number of Africans imported as agricultural slaves grew enormously, becoming a fundamental element for the economy and the social system that had to find a formalization. The laws relating to their status, political and social legal were thus defined even before the American War of Independence. Formally, the slaves of America enjoyed certain rights, as in the case of private property. However, these were rights that the slave owner was not obliged to respect, and they were isolated cases. In general, fundamental human rights were violated continuously. Slaves could, for example, be sexually abused by their masters; families could be separated because their members were sold to different plantations; brutal treatments such as mutilation and murder, theoretically forbidden by Law, remained quite common until the 19th century. Slave owners were then prohibited from teaching them to read.

A brief history of the Indian wars in the U.S.A.

The Indian wars are wars fought between the 17th and 19th centuries, by the native Indians of North America against the European colonizers and the government forces of the United States of America, to prevent them from being settled on their own territories. Divisions existing between the Indian "nations" with the inadequacy of the means at their disposal, reduced the clash to a long chain of defeats and massacres of the natives, interrupted by victories, which immediately became a legend because of their exceptionality.

In the early nineteenth century, the head of the Shawnee, Tecumseh, managed to organize a confederation of Indian nations that alarmed the governor of the Territory of Indiana, William Henry Harrison. In 1811 Harrison resumed hostilities and, at the battle of Tippecanoe, defeated the Confederation. The conflict was part of the war of 1812, with the Indians on the British side. The death of Tecumseh (October 1813) caused the disintegration of the Confederation, and the main tribes signed peace with the Americans.

The Indian Removal Act of 1830 drastically solved the "problem." Entire Indian nations were driven out of their homelands and deported west of the Mississippi: Sauk, Fox,

19

Creek, Cherokee, and Semolina tribes tried in vain to resist, but by the end of the 1850s all Indian presence in the eastern part of the U.S.A. had disappeared. Between 1840 and 1890, the federal government organized a system of reserves within which to force the Indian nations, thus beginning the conquest and colonization of western territories.

In the mid-century, Bannock and Shoshone of Oregon and Idaho, Ute of Nevada and Utah, Apache, and Navajo of the southeastern territories joined forces in a vast but ineffective attempt at rebellion. Between the sixties and seventies, Arapaho, Cheyenne, and Sioux entered a war fought with particular ferocity on both sides, during which took place the mythical battle of Little Bighorn (June 25, 1876), during which the 7th Cavalry Regiment, led by General Custer, was annihilated by Cheyenne and Sioux of Sitting Bull and Crazy Horse, both forced to surrender within a year. The last extensive resistance action was conducted in the 1880s by the Apaches of Geronimo. On December 29, 1890, with the massacre of Wounded Knee, in South Dakota, where the Federal Cavalry slaughtered Sioux men, women, and children, the Indian wars came to an end.

Ku Klux Klan

The Ku Klux Klan (also known as K.K.K.) was born in the late 1800s in the United States to advocate the superiority of the white race. The history of this American Movement can be divided into three periods:

- ✓ from 1865 to 1874 when it developed as a brotherhood of former soldiers in the Confederate States Army of America;
- ✓ from 1915 to 1944 when it became a real movement;
- ✓ from the postwar period until today, when the group becomes a series of small organizations.

The Ku Klux Klan was created in Pulaski, in Tennessee, on the night of December 24, 1865, by a group of young people from a good local society of veterans of the Confederate Army. None of them imagined that the group would become one of the leading organizations of American racism.

Warning on the inferiority of blacks, and therefore not recognizing their civil and political rights, the members of the Klan (Klansmen) undertook to obstruct the action of the Reconstruction governments formed after 1867. The Klansmen were covered in white tunics and masked by long pointed hoods. They began to terrorize federal officers to push them to leave their posts, as well as the more enterprising blacks, to prevent them from exercising their newly acquired political rights or carrying out public activity. To this purpose, threats were followed by flogging and mutilation, up to murder.

But what does Ku Klux Klan mean? The etymology of the name is uncertain, but according to some, it could derive from the Greek *kuklos*, "circle," and from the *clan*, "family."

The group took on greater importance after the Nashville convention, which took place in the summer of 1867, during which General Nathan Bedford Forrest was awarded the title of "Great Wizard." The organization wanted on the one hand, to help widows and war orphans, and on the other, to oppose the extension of voting rights to blacks.

In 1869 Forrest then dissolved the confraternity because he thought it had strayed too far from its original goals. In 1871 American President Ulysses Simpson Grant signed the "Klan Act and Enforcement Act," by which the organization was declared an illegal terrorist group. The Act also authorized the use of force to defeat the activities of the brotherhood. The document was then declared unconstitutional in 1882. However, it had served to eliminate the organization from many countries in the United States in those years.

The second phase of the Ku Klux Klan developed during the First World War when many whites began to think that black people, Jewish bankers, and other minorities were the primary cause of the country's economic problems. The founder of this second phase was in 1915 William J. Simmons, who also introduced the new symbol of the organization: the burning cross.

In addition to African Americans, Catholics and Jews also became the object of the Klan's intimidation. The wave of violence reached its peak in the 1920s, especially in the southern states.

This second phase of the organization began to lose consensus during the 1930s, and in 1944 the organization was dissolved again. In the 1920s and 1930s, a subsection of the organization also spread, called the Black Legion. It operated in the Midwest and is remembered for the violence of its attacks, especially against socialists and communists. After the Second World War, many groups took over the name Ku Klux Klan to indicate their opposition to the Civil Rights Movement. Some of these groups are still active.

Ku Klux Klan as a symbol

Since 1915, members of the Ku Klux Klan could be recognized by the white tunics they wore. A white cone-shaped hood was also used to hide the face, with holes for the eyes. According to some explanations, this "uniform" was chosen to intimidate the blacks, who considered those masks as the materialization of the spirits of the Southern soldiers who died during the war of secession, returned to earth to take revenge and punish their enemies. According to other explanations, the tunic was the symbol of humility because the task they had to perform had been assigned to them directly by God, and they had to do it in the best way possible while maintaining anonymity.

Ku Klux Klan today

There are at least three groups still active that can be traced back to the Ku Klux Klan:

- Knights of the Ku Klux Klan, the Knights of the Ku Klux Klan

- Imperial Klan of America, the Imperial Klan of America

- Brotherhood of Klans Knights, the Brotherhood of the Knights of the Klan.

These are extreme right-wing groups of racist ideology and anti-Catholic matrix. It is estimated that in 2018 the number of members affiliated to the Klan ranged between 8000 and 12000.

With the strengthening of the civil rights movement in the 1950s and 1960s, the Klan attempted to relaunch itself as an advanced and radical point of opposition to racial integration. At the end of the Eighties, it was made up of about fifteen organizations, with an overall follow up estimated at 5000 units.

CHAPTER 2 - CIVIL RIGHTS MOVEMENTS

In 1877, the political leaders of the North withdrew the federal troops of the southern states: it is the "1877 compromise", in which the police state in the South begins. Between 1890 and 1905, the South emanated the complex of segregationist laws.

Over the years, many organizations were founded to assert the civil rights of the black population and to counter the abuses and injustices suffered.

NNBL

In Boston, Booker T.Washington organizes the National Negro Business League (NNBL), aimed at the development of the black bourgeoisie.

Booker T.Washington was one of the first figures in the struggle for the civil rights of black people. Of humble origins, he was freed from slavery as a child, but he managed to redeem himself thanks to good education at Hempton University. He became the director of an institution reserved for African Americans who wanted to become teachers. He believed that knowledge was the key to redemption for every African-American citizen. To this end, he was able to obtain a lot of funding for his school, managing to pay for the education of many black children in the South of the United States. He also funded many lawsuits against racial segregation. He was the first African American to be invited to the White House in Washington.

NAACP

In 1909 the National Association for the Advancement of Coloured People (NAACP) was founded as one of the most influential civil rights associations in the United States.

The statute of the association was founded to "promote equal rights and caste or eradicate racial prejudice among citizens of member states; to advance the interests of colored citizens; to guarantee them impartial suffrage; and to increase their opportunities to ensure justice in court, education for children, employment according to their ability, and complete equality before the law."

Till today, it is one of the best-known associations in the United States. Over the years, it has expanded its mission to ensure political, educational, social, and economic equality of rights for all people and to eliminate discrimination based on race, taking into account issues such as police misconduct, the status of black foreign refugees, and economic development questions.

One of its founders was William Edward Burghardt Du Bois (known as W. E. B. Du Bois). Du Bois came to national prominence as the leader of the Niagara Movement, another organization founded in 1905 by a group of African-American activists who wanted equal rights for black people. The Niagara Movement disbanded four years later, while a group of whites organized the National Negro Committee.

Other organizations

In 1911 some whites founded the N.U.L. (National Urban League) for the inclusion of black people in industrial production. Two years later, in Newark, **Noble Drew Ali** founded the *Moorish American Science Temple*, while **Carter G. Woodson** founded the Association for the *Study of Negro Life and History*. A significant date was 1917 when **Marcus Garvey** founded the *Unia (Universal Negro Improvement Association)* for the separation between Blacks and Whites and the "return" of blacks to Africa. It will have up to 3 million members and, during the First World War, it will become the first black popular Movement with mass characteristics.

In 1919, the Commission on Interracial Cooperation was funded. In 1944, it was transformed into the Southern Regional Council, to reconcile the contrasts which exploded in the South, when the black veterans of the World War (in which 342.000 had participated, with 100.000 fighters at the front) pretended to "boast" of the ribbons of veterans. Twelve years later, W.D. Fard founded the Nation of Islam (Black Muslims) and appointed its first pastor, **Elijah Muhammad**, who became head of the group in 1934. In 1933 the Southern Conference for Human Welfare was founded, whose educational sector became autonomous under the name of SCEF (Southern Conference Educational Fund). The National Negro Congress was founded in 1935, an organization aimed at uniting all the Negro unions and associations. A. Philip Randolph, President of The Brotherhood of Sleeping Car Porters (BSCP), takes over the presidency.

In 1940 the majority of members joined the *Pullman Company*, one of the largest companies that employed black people. After a year, Randolph proposes a march of negroes on Washington; the Movement of the march on Washington against discrimination in the war industries was born.

After World War II

Between 1940 and 1960, black people living outside the 11 states of the old Confederation increased by more than twice, i.e., from less than 4 million in 1940, to more than 9 million in 1960: representing roughly half the entire black population in the U.S. This increase was concentrated in the 12 largest cities in the U.S., which hosted between a quarter and a third of African Americans. In the cities of Washington and New York, Blacks make up the majority of the population. In Detroit, Baltimore, Cleveland, and St. Louis, they were more than a third. In many other cities such as Chicago, Philadelphia, Cincinnati, Indianapolis, and Oakland, they far exceed the fourth. In 1943, the Congress of Racial Equality (CORE) was founded. After the Nazi aggression against the USSR, the first black organizations agreed on the opportunity for the blacks to enlist: their number rose from 115,197 in 1941 to 1,174,000, and about one million were engaged in the war industries.

CHAPTER 3: MALCOLM X

A character who played a fundamental role in the racist America of the first half of the 20th century, fighting, until his assassination, for the rights of blacks, was Malcolm Little. He soon changed his name to Malcolm X. He was born in Omaha, Nebraska, on May 19, 1925, a time when the United States was in full racial segregation. His father Earl abandoned him very soon because he was killed in 1931 by a group of "white supremacy" supporters. His mother Louise Little, who was judged legally unsound, was forced to watch her eleven children being taken away from her. After completing his studies at junior high school, and achieving the best results in his class, he dropped out when her favorite teacher bluntly told him that becoming a renowned lawyer was "not a realistic goal for a nigger," he saw alcohol and violence as the only means of survival. During his youth, Malcolm experienced the brutality of racism and segregation on his own skin. He reacted to it with feelings of hatred and revenge, which consumed his energy for much of his adolescence. Malcolm was imprisoned in a harsh prison in Nebraska in 1946 when he was accused of theft, where he met a black American who gave him his first rebirth. He, of Islamic religion, introduced Malcolm to the same faith by making him convert to Islam, and teaching him all about the venerable Elijah Mohammad, founder of the "Nation of Islam" (N.O.I.). "It was as if a great light had entered my life; it dazzled me," Malcolm tells later. In the period following his conversion, Malcolm became an avid reader and enriched his vocabulary by transcribing an entire dictionary.

As soon as he was released from prison, Malcolm X went to Elijah Muhammad in Chicago. It was during this period that he received the surname "X" to symbolize the rejection of his "slave surname" and the absence of a real African-Muslim surname, "The surname Little represents the surname that the slavers imposed on my ancestors who came from Africa in chains. Who am I? What is my real last name? No one can know, so X", Malcolm explained. The camp of the "Nation of Islam" soon realized his extraordinary qualities, and initially entrusting him with important tasks within the sect. Later, he was named the organizer of the activities, thus making him famous throughout the United States and abroad. Malcolm X was endowed with great charisma. His word, charged with inner tension, was very active on the spectators, and so he gave numerous speeches in which he spoke about the pain and suffering caused to African Americans by the white man, and the need to react to this situation; not to try at all costs to look like white people, but to feel proud to be black. In 1958, he married Betty, whom he met within the "Nation of Islam," and who was the first to open Malcolm's eyes to the ambiguous figure of Elija Mohammad. It was on March 12, 1964, after Malcolm X had been a follower and supporter of Elijah Mohammed for twelve years. During that time, he became in turn racist towards the "white man." Due to the sect rivalries and the double-crossing that his leader was doing, he decided to leave the Nation of Islam. Malcolm later gave a speech, known as the "Declaration of Independence," in which he explained that his separation would not change his thinking on the racial issue, but that "now that I have more freedom of action, I want to use it to develop more articulated instruments of common action." He then expressed his intentions about wanting to collaborate with all the black leaders, despite their previous differences, asking them to forget his negative appreciation as he had done about theirs, since a universal solution to a problem that concerned everyone had to be found. He was still convinced that the resolution was the return home of all the black people. However, this was a "long-term program," and during the time necessary to implement it, they had to assert their rights to allow them to live on an equal footing with the whites. Malcolm X, therefore, stated that it was right and legitimate for a black man to defend himself if attacked by whites.

Malcolm announced the birth of a new mosque in New York City, the "Muslim Mosque Inc.," in which all religious blacks could participate. At the same time, whites were not allowed to join. Later, Malcolm was initiated to the meaning of true Islam by Dr. Mahmud Yussef Shawarbi, which appeared very different from the one propagated by racist sects like the Nation of Islam;

"you will not be a true Muslim until you wish for others what you want for yourself. "

He was so impressed and disturbed by these words that he decided to go on a pilgrimage to Mecca, an action that every true Muslim had to do at least once in his life, and he returned profoundly changed by this experience. In Mecca, he knew the true spirit of brotherhood and freedom, but the thing that shocked him most was that there were no distinctions either for blacks or whites or any kind of race. He found himself in prayer with the whites he detested so much because of the influence Elijah Mohammed had exerted on him, so much so that when he returned from this trip, he said: "In Saudi Arabia, I experienced a spirit of unity and brotherhood."

On his return from Mecca, Malcolm X decided to call himself Al-Hajj Malik al Shabbaz, and, "lit up with a new spiritual light," he fought for human and civil rights with even greater determination. His message was no longer addressed exclusively to blacks in American ghettos, but also to intellectuals in the elegant suburbs. His words were addressed to men of all colors and races, but he knew that in doing so, he was exposing himself to considerable risks. The press kept him under constant pressure, and he received death threats more and more often. However, he stood in his way and was not discouraged, knowing that the end would come at any moment. In one of his last speeches, he wrote, "I know that society has often murdered those who tried to change it, and if I die having brought some light, having exposed an obvious truth that will help eliminate the cancer of racism from the body of America, then all the merits will belong to God, and only the mistakes will be mine. I am not a racist and do not believe in any of the principles of racism. I don't believe in any form of segregation or discrimination."

On February 14, 1965, Malcolm and his family survived an attack on their home, which was set on fire during the night. A week later, on February 21, during a public address in Manhattan, three black men struck him with various firearms. He died within moments. It is still uncertain today whether the perpetrators of this murder should be sought in the Nation of Islam or other organizations.

The life and history of Malcolm X have greatly influenced the evolution of the African American community and beyond. Malcolm's death, so early and sudden, led many African Americans to rediscover their roots. Many became Muslim, adopted Muslim names, and explored the culture of their ancestors' country. Even the Nation of Islam", under the guidance of Elijah Mohammad's son, converted to Orthodox Islam, leaving fanaticism and violence aside.

CHAPTER 4: WOMEN ACTIVISTS

Rosa Parks

At the beginning of December 1955, a black woman, Rosa Parks, refuses to give her place on a bus to a white man; she was arrested. The black community (50,000 people), led by Martin Luther King, then head of the NAACP, organizes the boycott against segregated buses: it will last 381 days.

Rosa Parks was an African-American woman from Montgomery, the capital of Alabama. The scenario of our history is, therefore, the deep South of the United States of America, where laws imposed racial segregation in public places, including buses.

On December 1, 1955, Rosa Parks got on a public transport that would take her home after a day's work at the Montgomery Fair department store. After paying for her ticket, Rosa took her seat in front of the black zone, halfway down the bus, flanked by three other black passengers. At the next stop, some white passengers occupied the front seats, but one of the white passengers remained standing; it was at that point that the driver ordered the black passengers to give up their seats: everyone obeyed except Rosa. At that point, the driver of the vehicle called the police who arrested the woman who, unlike what is written very imprecisely in some textbooks, was not an older woman, but was only 42 years old and came from a family with a great tradition of civil rights activism.

It is clear that her gesture was not impromptu, but the result of a convinced political militancy, which often led her to denounce segregation in the buses. That gesture had enormous political repercussions, perhaps unforeseen by Parks herself. The black community of Montgomery had lit the fuse of the boycott. Last but not least, Parks had the brilliant idea of normalizing the event with the entirely successful aim of amplifying the effects of the occasion: "I didn't get on a bus to be arrested," Rosa said. I got on the bus to go home".

Born in the small town of Tuskegee in Alabama in 1913, Rosa Parks was a sympathizer of Marcus Garvey's Universal Association for the Improvement of the Blacks, and her family of origin was an active member of the African Episcopal Methodist Church. The latter institution was an organization that often stood up in protest against segregation. In 1900, for example, black pastors urged their assemblies to boycott the city's tram system in protest against discrimination on public transportation.

Rosa's awareness of racism issues came from a very early age, as she recalls: "We talked about the fact that if the Klan men threatened to break into our house, we would go to bed dressed to be ready to run away in case of danger.

From 1931, Rosa lived with her husband, Raymond Parks, who was a white-skinned man. The man was also a civil rights activist, more specifically from the Montgomery section of the National Association for the Advancement of Colored People (NAACP).

In 1941, one of the turning points in Rosa's life took place since she was hired at the Maxwell Field military base, thanks to the measures of integration within the military bases, wanted by President Franklin D. Roosevelt. Rosa herself recalled: "You could say that Maxwell opened my eyes. I could get on a tram integrated into the base, but when I got off it, I had to go home on the segregated buses.

Also, in those months, Parks became secretary of the NACCP in Montgomery, spending August 1955 organizing a meeting with Martin Luther King, in which the leader spoke of the 1954 Brown ruling by the Supreme Court against segregation in schools. Parks was also present and commented: "You can't imagine happiness without an agreement between blacks and whites. It is a time of great hope.

In 1954 and 1955, Parks worked for the white couple Clifford and Virginia Durr, who introduced Rosa to the Highlander Folk School, which became a center of study for black rights during those two years.

In 1955 the tension in Montgomery was very high because of a murder of a black man who had disobeyed some bus drivers, and in October of the same year, an 18-year-old boy was imprisoned for not giving the seat to a white woman. He, therefore, expected an excuse in an atmosphere already full of social tensions. In particular, civil rights associations were hoping for massive support from the black women of Montgomery, who did not own a car and were the primary users of public transport.

The black community was ready for collective action, and it is certainly wrong to speak of spontaneous reaction by Rosa, who had undoubtedly been planning the boycott for some time. An activist with her background could certainly not stand up at the request of an explicitly racist driver. As for Parks, she was found guilty of breaking the segregationist laws and condemned by a court of Law: the black community responded with a boycott to the bitter end, until the authorities changed the provisions.

The boycott would last one year until economic pressure from the municipality restored bus transport. As for Parks' position, the boycott cost her a job at Montgomery Fair, while Raymond, her comrade, preferred to quit his role in the Air Force because of the constant threats of dismissal. The Parks were surrounded in many ways: the landlord increased the rent, and the couple received continuous death threats.

Due to the impossibility of finding a job, the Parks moved to Detroit, but Rosa continued to follow the activism of their hometowns and continued to participate in the rallies. Parks' popularity did not diminish, and her iconic status is evidenced by her meeting with Nelson Mandela in Detroit in 1975, sealed by a long and silent embrace between the two.

The history of activism would not be the same without the famous Parks arrest, combined with some fortuitous combination: Mrs. Parks' arrest was well linked to the subsequent boycott promoted by Martin Luther King. The black churches also had a prolonged boycott activity in Baton Rouge, and Rosa Parks had been very sensitive to civil rights sermons.

For some time, the NAACP had been raising public awareness of the plight of blacks, counting numerous victories in defense of many blacks accused of funding the cause of the Montgomery bus boycott. It was not forgotten that there were many associations, such as the Highlander Folk School, which were stimulated by Rosa Parks' action.

In essence, the boycott was rooted in deep-rooted practices of social conflict, as Rosa has repeatedly pointed out: "I find that if I am overthinking about my problems and the fact that sometimes things are not the way I want them to be, I do not make any progress. But if I look around and see what I can do, and I do it, I progress".

In a profile on Rosa Parks, it is worth mentioning the experience of two women who fought for civil rights:

- **Ella Baker (1903-1986)** and Fannie Lou Hamer (1917-1977). The former was an organizer always active in extraordinary events, with a career that spanned fifty years. She fought alongside many of the most famous civil rights leaders of the 20th century, including W.E.B. Du Bois, Thurgood Marshall, A. Philip Randolph, and Martin Luther King. He was also a guide for many budding activists such as Diane Nash, Stokely Carmichael, Bob Moses, and Parks herself. Baker fought for radical democracy, and her militancy was described as "one of the most important African American leaders of the 20th century and the most influential woman in the civil rights movement".

- **Lou Hamer** was a women's rights activist, a soul for the black community, and a leader in the civil rights movement. She was co-founder and vice president of the Democratic Party for Freedom, whose interests she represented at the 1964 National Democratic Convention.

`Linda Brown, a symbol of equality in U.S. schools`

Linda Brown, a 9-year-old girl, in 1951 found herself at the center of the "Brown v. Ministry of Education" lawsuit that would end African-American school segregation in America.

It was her father Oliver, who, faced with his daughter's refusal to enroll in summer classes at Monroe Elementary School, a white school in Topeka, Kansas, sued the local school authority along with four other families. In this way, a process was set in motion that would allow a "normal" schoolgirl, like so many others in the U.S.A., to introduce such a significant transformation in that country.

The Supreme Court, in fact, on May 17, 1954, decreed that "separate educational structures are inherently unjust," a violation of the 14th Amendment of the American Constitution, which states that by Law, no citizen may be denied equal protection.

It was Thurgood Marshall, a lawyer with the National Association for the Advancement of Black People (NAACP), operating in the United States in defense of civil rights, who argued the case before the Supreme Court; later, Marshall himself became the first African-American judge of that body.

Linda was described by many as "representing a group of young heroes who, together with their families, fought and ended segregation in state schools. A not smooth action, a sacrifice that broke barriers and changed the meaning of equality in the country.

When Linda was a child, middle and high schools were already integrated, while primary schools, including "Monroe," were not. To reach the bus that took her two miles away to the black school, she and her sisters had to cross the railway and a bustling road: a danger and suffering, especially in the winter months. Here lies the origin of her father's judicial struggle.

Linda Brown, however, is not only an essential name in the history of civil rights in America. Her contribution to the life of the community in which she lived leaves a legacy that goes beyond all that. For years she played the piano in the Church of which she was a part and taught children to play that instrument.

"She was a spiritual woman," they say of her, "who loved not only the Lord but also her family and community, and who was able to take responsibility for the cause she won. In expressing its condolences, the NAACP called Brown "a heroine of our nation" for whom she will always remain eternally grateful.

Ruby Bridges

Ruby Bridges was the first black girl to enter a class of only white pupils at the age of 6. Until then, there were no mixed classes, and whites were strictly separated from African Americans, who could not attend the same institutions as their white peers.

It was November 14, 1960, and the school was the William Frantz Elementary School in New Orleans. Ruby Bridges, appeared in class escorted by a group of federal agents, greeted by an angry mob, who rebelled by throwing objects at the girl. The little girl was not accompanied by any sweet look, in what was supposed to be, as for all children, a critical moment to cherish in their hearts. Waiting for her, was only an army of war that rejected her. In class, she was not welcomed by any comrade or teacher. The parents of her classmates withdrew their children that day, and the teachers refused to give lessons to a little black girl, for society, destined to live on the margins of all things.

Unfortunately, from then on, the life of little Ruby Bridges and her family was punctuated by threats and retaliation. They were forced to live under constant escort as their lives were severely threatened. Not only that, the hatred questioned the tranquil life of the family. They were deprived of everything, even the necessary. The father was fired, and the mother was prohibited from shopping in certain food stores. The grandparents were also denied the land they cultivated as sharecroppers.

Ruby Bridges was allowed to study and learn by a single teacher, the only one who did not evade, and she volunteered to accompany the child. For a long time, little Ruby Bridges was forced to bring food from home to avoid the danger of poisoning. In the days and months that followed, Ruby Bridges was insulted and threatened on several occasions, but due to the proximity of other black and white families, the Bridges resisted, and little Ruby won her battle.

As an adult, she will say, *"Don't follow the path, go where there is no road and create it."*

Angela Davis

She is a well-known activist of the African American movement in the United States, which has dedicated her life to fighting all forms of racism and social injustice.

Born in January 1944 in Birmingham, Angela Davis, from an early age, finds herself confronted with racial conflicts, as her neighborhood is known for episodes of intense tension. In adolescence, she approached communist and socialist ideologies, beginning to study at the Little Red School House, known for its progressive positions. He also started to serve in the military for a communist student group. Later, she moved to Europe, where her studies led her to a growing civil consciousness and awareness. The civil rights movement that was rampant in the United States prompted her to return home so she could be at the forefront of fighting social injustice.

Because of her activism, Davis was linked to the episode of August 7, 1960, when Jonathan Jackson, during a trial against some Black Panther Party militant inmates, drew his gun in the courtroom and took the judge and some jurors hostage. In the shooting, the kidnappers and the judge were killed. The weapons used by Jackson were registered in the name of Angela Davis, and under California law, the person who buys the guns used in a crime is guilty of it. During her time in prison, Davis wrote a lot, and those pages gave life to her most famous and revolutionary writings.

After the harsh imprisonment, Davis was acquitted of the charges and returned to fight social injustice even harder, focusing more on the situation of the prisoners, and particularly on detentions whose origins lie in racial reasons.

In addition to being part of the Communist Party, Angela Davis took part in the Black Panther Party. According to Davis, the working class had the task and duty to fight oppression and racial conflict.

Now famous for her political activities and her writings, she was called to teach History of Consciousness at the University of Santa Cruz, and to this day, she continues to fight for civil rights.

Many songs were dedicated to her revolutionary actions, such as *Angela* by John Lennon and Yoko Ono and *Sweet Black Angel* by the Rolling Stones. Her courage and devotion have inspired millions of people, to the point of striking the souls of the greatest artists of all time.

"I am no longer accepting the things I cannot change. I am changing the things I cannot accept."

- ○ Angela Y. Davis

CHAPTER 5: PEACEFUL PROTESTS

The Greensboro Sit-Ins

In February 1960, in a café in Greensboro, four university students were refused a coffee they had asked for: they continued to sit down, and the idea of a sit-in was born. By May, more than 90 black and white students will have been there.

***

"Jump, black crow, jump" was sung in the South by racist minstrels with their faces painted black smoke, "jump Jim Crow" when the white man ordered you to. And they jumped, until that day in February 1960, when four "crows" refused to drop, perched on bar stools, and did not move for weeks. All it took was that gesture, and that simple sit in, that simple sitting, to change a story that half a century later would bring one of them to the White House.

The first sit-in, a non-violent protest technique that for generations would have marked the era of civil disobedience, seems like a historical anecdote from a yellowed memory album today, and is instead a chronicle of yesterday. In North Carolina in 1960, a year and a half before the election of John F. Kennedy, segregationist laws still reigned, which the white lords of the South had hurried to impose after the abolition of slavery.

It was in North Carolina, one of the untamed fortresses of segregation, that four black students, not even twenty years old, dared the unthinkable. In Greensboro, they sat at the counter of the restaurant inside the Woolworth emporium, the sanctuary of shopping, and the place where customers stopped for a quick bite between purchases. "They don't serve niggers here," a waitress tried to remove them, using the most brutal and offensive expression, because that's what the state law, municipal ordinances, and the internal regulations of the bar wanted. The four, who since then, and forever passed into civil rights legend as the "Greensboro Four" did not move. They remained seated.

They had neither prepared nor arranged anything; the "Forbidden Four," Joseph McNeil, Ezell Blair Jr., David Richmond, and Franklin McCain, simply decided that they had had enough of being treated like infected animals to keep them in quarantine with the "separate but equal" ruse that still attempts, in its apparent clarity, racist and xenophobic all over the world. They had had enough of not being able to drink at the same fountains reserved for white people, not being able to use the same bathrooms, not being able to eat the food often cooked by their brothers. Or as Rosa Parks had done five years earlier in Montgomery, Alabama, to be forced to sit in the back rows of public buses, bought and paid for with their taxes. But the non-violent, Gandhian rebellion of Martin Luther King, of Rosa

Parks, had subsided, and had lost steam until that February 1955, when the four students sat down to ask for a hamburger. Within a few days, the new technique of sit-in, of sitting down, of offering passive resistance, of not committing violent or vandalistic acts and leaving it to the white authorities to use truncheons, handcuffs, dogs and fire hydrants to remove them, spread with the force of a fire in the Prairie. In the other cities of the South where the "Law of the Raven" was in power, the apartheid, Selma, Montgomery, Atlanta, Nashville, and Memphis, students, kitchen workers, cleaning women and men of toil, entered simultaneously in the restaurants, in the supermarkets, in the department stores where the counter for a quick breakfast was in rigor and sat down. It was in Greensboro, where the first American sit-down took place that the wall of segregation began to collapse. Dozens of other black boys swarmed through the streets of Downtown, entering the shops and stores, without shouting, without waving signs, just to sit down. And it was not justice, or shame, or modesty of their own anachronism that moved the good citizens of South Carolina. It was the green God, the dollar. When business on the Downtown streets collapsed, the shopkeepers and owners of the then formidable Woolworth chain gave in. Without changing the laws, they quietly began serving burgers, fries, and ketchup to the hated "niggers" and opening the toilets to them. Four more years, and the murder of a president in office in Dallas, would have to pass for the surrender of the Greensboro merchants to become the "Civil Rights Act" signed by Lyndon Johnson in 1964. Three boys coming down from the North should have been killed in Mississippi so that that Law and that right to vote would not be emptied by the cooperation between sheriffs, mayors, and K.K.K. But the Wall of the Black Crow had fallen.

The Freedom Riders

In 1961, on Easter Eve, in Raleigh, the 1st Southern Students' Convention was held and organized by SCLC, and the SNCC (Student Nonviolent Coordinating Committee) was founded. The CORE organized the first Freedom Riders to abolish segregation in the waiting rooms of southern public transport.

The Freedom Riders traveled on the buses of the Greyhound lines to demonstrate against the hostility of the Southern States to implement the judgments by the Supreme Court that declared unconstitutional racial segregation on means of transport, in waiting rooms, and restaurants. In particular, a Court decision in 1960 contravened Jim Crow's 1876 laws that imposed segregation and were in force in many states. The first bus left on May 4, 1961; then, there were others through Virginia, Georgia, Tennesee, Alabama, Mississippi, and Louisiana. Onboard, thirteen men and women, black and white sitting next to each other.

On May 14, 1961, the Freedom Riders bus was set on fire, and its passengers were beaten by an angry mob of white racist Ku Klux Klan members. It was Mother's Day; the bus had just arrived in Anniston, Alabama. The driver tried to leave the station quickly, but the bus was reached. The attackers attempted to block the exits to trap the passengers who managed to escape. They were chased and savagely beaten.

After the bus fire on May 14, despite the presence of the police, a group of protesters attacked the Freedom Riders with sticks and baseball bats at Montgomery station. It was May 21, 1961, and 600 feds were sent into the city to stop the violence. The next day Martin Luther King spoke to a thousand supporters of the activists. The protest even broke into the Church. The civil rights leader demanded urgent action from Robert Kennedy, who ordered the use of tear gas to disperse the crowd. Martial Law was introduced, and the National Guard was charged with bringing order. The bus continued its journey in a crescendo of aggression and violence that culminated on May 24 with a mass arrest of the activists on their arrival in Jackson. More buses arrived and continued the arrests until the city's prisons were filled. The attention of the press began to raise awareness in the American public. The Freedom Riders' non-violent protest did not stop and thus began to prepare the ground for the great March on Washington for work and freedom on August 28, 1963.

The Selma to Montgomery Marches

On March 7, 1965, hundreds of peaceful protesters were attacked by the Alabama police. It was a turning point in the struggle for the civil rights of black Americans.

The police joined groups of volunteer citizens and attacked six hundred people who were demonstrating peacefully on the Edmund Pettus Bridge in the town of Selma. Without any provocation, the police loaded the protesters on horseback, hit them with sticks, and threw tear gas at them. Dozens of people were injured, and the images of the clashes went around the world. It was one of the most critical moments in the struggle for the civil rights of black Americans and led the then President of the United States, Lyndon Johnson, to enact the Voting Rights Act. This Law banned racial discrimination in elections and is considered one of the most significant achievements of the civil rights movement today.

As we already know, at the time of Selma's clashes, racial segregation was still in force. Blacks enjoyed only limited political and civil rights, and could not vote. The set of laws that did not allow them to vote was identified under the name of "Jim Crow": they were rules dating back to the years immediately following the American Civil War, which ended in 1865. At the time, the federal government had imposed an end to slavery on rebel states in the South. In an attempt to limit the effects of slave liberation, southern politicians had introduced

"Jim Crow" laws that effectively made the black people into second-class citizens. For nearly a century, the Supreme Court rejected all appeals against these laws. Then, in 1964, President Johnson imposed the "Civil Rights Act," which made discrimination on racial, religious, and sexual grounds illegal. In many states, however, the laws that prevented black people from voting remained in force.

Between 1964 and early 1965, there were many demonstrations across the United States organized by the civil rights movement to demand implementation of the Civil Rights Act and to claim the right to vote. The police often responded very harshly, and violent clashes were frequent. In February 1965, a civil rights demonstration was held in the city of Marion, Alabama: at a certain point, the street lighting was turned off, and the police charged the demonstrators. One of the people who were participating in the protest, Jimmie Lee Jackson, took refuge in a café with his mother and was joined by two officers. There was a clash, and Jackson was shot twice in the stomach. Eight days later, Jackson died at the Selma City Hospital from an infection caused by the wound.

In response to the incident, several civil rights organizations decided to organize a march from Selma, where Jackson had died, to Montgomery, the capital of Alabama. The purpose of the demonstration was to try to force the governor of the state, George Wallace, to answer for the clashes that had led to

Jackson's death. Also, as with the other demonstrations in those months, the organizers hoped to draw media attention to the continuing violations of black people's constitutional rights and accelerate the federal government's efforts to end segregation in the southern states. Wallace said the march was a risk to public safety and ordered local authorities to do everything possible to stop it.

Jim Clark, the county sheriff, obeyed very harshly. In addition to gathering all the police at his disposal, he issued an order requiring all white males over the age of 21 to report to the local court so they could be appointed deputy sheriff. On the morning of March 7, Clark was ready to oppose the demonstration, along with dozens of police officers and gangs of citizens armed with sticks.

As predicted by the organizers, the march started from the town of Selma, and about six hundred people, in a row of two, began to move along the highway 80 towards Montgomery. After a few hundred meters, they arrived at the Edmund Pettus bridge. At the exit of the bridge, Clark and his men had positioned themselves. Those who were at the beginning of the procession tried to talk to the policemen, without success: the demonstrators had to disperse immediately, the police said. Moments later, the cops started shoving the protesters. The first in line was thrown to the ground, those behind them began to back away and then to run, trying to get back on the bridge. The police started to hit them with sticks, while other officers on horseback loaded the fleeing protesters onto the deck, and other officers fired tear gas into the crowd. A total of 17 protesters were hospitalized.

The other marches

The demonstration was attended by dozens of journalists, and the clashes were filmed by several cameras. The images of the violence went around the world. In particular, the photo of Amelia Boynton, who had been shot unconscious on the ground, ended up on the covers of many newspapers. Police brutality turned almost immediately against the governor of Alabama. Johnson immediately condemned the clashes, as did all leaders of the civil rights movement.

Two days later, Martin Luther King should have conducted another march along the same bridge. Once again, the purpose of the demonstration was to reach Montgomery and the governor's palace, but again a court order forbade demonstrators to complete the march. King and the others still managed to gather 2,500 people. They crossed the Selma Bridge and united in prayer at the scene of the clashes in front of the riot police, refusing to continue to Montgomery. That same evening, members of the Klu Klux Klan attacked and killed one of the leaders of the march.

What was happening in Selma had now attracted the attention of the whole country and much of the world. In the following days, King and the other leaders of the Movement organized the third march to Montgomery. This time they managed to get all the necessary permits to get to the state capital. On March 25, in the last leg of the march, 25,000 people arrived under the bleachers of the Alabama Governor's Palace, where King gave one of his most famous speeches. Ten days earlier, on March 15, President Johnson had presented the *Voting Rights Act* to Congress. On August 6 of the same year, the Voting Rights Acts was converted into Law, officially ending legal discrimination against blacks throughout the United States.

***

The Laws of Jim Crow

These laws, enacted in individual southern states since 1876, helped to systematize racial segregation for blacks and members of ethnic groups other than whites. The separation was physical in schools, public places, on public transport, in restaurant bathrooms, and also had the precise objective of hindering the exercise of the right to vote by those who belonged to these communities.

As the presidential elections approach, in some American states, representatives of the Republican Party have proposed laws that, if passed, would complicate access to vote for specific categories of people: millions of citizens, especially young, poor, and African-Americans, who are traditionally close to the Democrats.

The most sensational case is that of Pennsylvania, where a law has been proposed that binds registration on electoral lists as a necessity for voting in the United States to the possession of a specific identification document: the driving license. If passed, this law will be applied to all voters regardless of the party they belong to. Still, only apparently it is intended to safeguard the electoral process from fraud (saying that the link between possession of a driving license and the exercise of the vote is not understood). If passed, the Law would prevent almost 759,000 people (9.2% of state voters) from voting: most of them live in urban areas, historically close to the Democrats, and more than 185,000 live in Philadelphia, where the Democrats are in the vast majority, and there is a large African-American community. Other similar laws have been proposed in a dozen American states, the majority of which are Republican-led.

The etymology of the expression "Jim Crow" is not clear. Still, it seems to be linked to "Jump Jim Crow," a popular song written in 1832 by Thomas Dartmouth Daddy Rice, a white comedian who played it in African-American make-up. From then on, "Jim Crow" became a derogatory expression to refer to African-Americans, and when the laws for racial segregation were enacted in 1838, they took this name. The phrase first appeared in the Dictionary of American English in 1904.

The so-called "Jim Crow" laws were passed mainly in the South of the country and especially by Democrats, who in the southern states retained more indulgences towards slavery and racism after the War of Secession. It was Florida that inaugurated the "Jim Crow" laws, which was once again administered by the Democrats after the war. In 1887, Florida approved the establishment of separate black and white compartment trains. From then on, the Democratic administrations of the former Confederation (the 11 southern states that had declared secession in 1861), supported by the Supreme Court, began to decline the most diverse forms of separation, seeking above all to limit the participation in the vote of the African-American community affected by poverty and illiteracy. They asked, for example, for a tax to vote, or they instituted evidence of general culture.

Woodrow Wilson, Democratic President of the South, gave a further boost to the "Jim Crow" laws by appointing many politicians in his government who were convinced segregationists. Racial segregation was also introduced in federal offices.

In the meantime, alongside the laws used by the states, a series of "private" regulations began to spread (in companies, parties, trade unions) to exclude blacks from society, preventing them, for example, from buying houses in specific neighborhoods and from entering or working in individual shops.

After the Second World War, the situation began to change. The Movement against segregation and civil rights organized strikes, protests, and marches. Democrats laboriously decided to support the cause. The Supreme Court began to rule that some laws and other forms of private discrimination were not constitutional. In 1944, for the first time, Justice Frank Murphy used the word "racism" in a court judgment.

The end of racial segregation by law coincided with the signing on July 2, 1964, by President Lyndon B. Johnson of the Civil Rights Act and, in 1965, of the Voting Rights Act: laws that declared illegal the inequality of registration on electoral rolls and racial segregation in public structures and that allowed the effective exercise of the right to vote for all and all without distinction of ethnicity and skin color.

***

Little Rock Nine

In 1957 in Arkansas, South of the United States, six black girls, and three black boys were allowed to enroll in Little Rock Public High School. The decision was made because of their excellent academic performance and aptitude test results as part of the attempt to forcibly integrate black and white people in the United States during those years. The boys were called the "Little Rock Nine," and their story was of central importance to the U.S. civil rights movement.

In 1954, in the United States, it was decided to put an end to racial segregation in schools. Before that year, black children and young people attended schools different from those of their white peers, even though there was no official ban on creating mixed classes. The situation was very critical, especially in the south of the United States, where racism was even more deeply rooted in society than in the northern states, and segregation seemed the only acceptable form of coexistence between whites and blacks.

September 4, 1957, in Little Rock, Arkansas, was the first day of school. The nine black boys had been selected to attend the city's high school, but troops of the Arkansas National Guard, acting on behalf of the state governor, prevented them from entering the classroom. The governor was Democrat Orval Faubus. The nine students were then driven away by verbal aggression from their white peers who, outraged at the idea that they were allowed into a "white" school, repelled them with insults and threats.

A few days later, President Eisenhower commissioned the Arkansas National Guard and sent federal troops to verify that the nine black boys were allowed to enter the school and to learn. Despite the presence of the army, the nine students were subjected to constant violence and discrimination acts by classmates, in front of teachers. The following summer, the governor of Arkansas, to postpone the gradual elimination of segregation, decided to suspend classes and close all schools under the excuse of continuous violence. A referendum endorsed the decision but, despite this, the families of the nine black boys and girls were held responsible by the rest of the population for the lost school year, and were consequently, victims of further attacks and discrimination. The government prohibited the opening of private schools for white students, and the following year the public school was reopened.

***

Richard e Mildred Loving

In 1958, 18-year-old Mildred became pregnant with Richard, and the two went to Washington, DC to get married, circumventing the laws of the state of Virginia that forbade mixed marriages. When they were back at their home in Central Point, Virginia, the Lovings had many problems. An anonymous caller reported the couple and the local police broke into their house in the middle of the night, hoping to surprise them during sexual intercourse (according to the laws of the state of Virginia, sexual intercourse between people of different "races" was also a crime). The Lovings were sleeping, and Mildred showed the police their marriage certificate, but the couple was tried anyway (Loving vs. Virginia case).

In fact, the police informed them that the marriage certificate was not valid. The following year the Lovings were sentenced to one year in prison because "they lived together as husband and wife contrary to the peace and dignity of the state;" the sentence would have been suspended if they had left Virginia and had not been back together for at least 25 years. So the Lovings moved to Washington DC, where they lived for five years in a kind of exile in their own country. Then, tired of not being able to visit their families as a couple, they decided to appeal and asked for help from the American Civil Liberties Union (ACLU). This association fought for civil rights. The ACLU assigned them two volunteer lawyers, Bernard S Cohen and Philip J Hirschkop, who brought their case, Loving vs. Virginia, from a local court in Virginia to the Supreme Court.

The Lovings did not attend the last hearing in Washington DC, but Richard Loving asked his lawyer to read a brief message in his place: "Mr. Cohen, tell the court that I love my wife and that it is unfair that I cannot live in Virginia with her. On June 12, 1967, the Supreme Court overturned the ruling unanimously. It ruled that the ban on mixed marriages was unconstitutional and contrary to the 14th Amendment of the Constitution, which reaffirmed equal rights to protect former slaves after the

Secession War. Despite the Supreme Court ruling, the laws against marriages were not abolished in some states; Alabama tightened them until 1970 and was the last state to adapt to the Court's decision in 2000. However, other mixed couples can marry thanks to the case won by the Lovings.

The Lovings had three children. Richard died at the age of 41 in 1975, hit by a drunk truck driver; in the same accident, Mildred lost her right eye, but survived and died at the age of 68 in 2008. Loving Day is still celebrated today on June 12, the anniversary of the historic ruling of 1967 that established the validity of Richard's marriage to Mildred.

CHAPTER 6: I HAVE A DREAM

Martin Luther King (Atlanta, Georgia 1929 - Memphis, Tennessee 1968), a Baptist cleric and U.S. politician, was one of the most influential leaders of the U.S. civil rights movement and a leading proponent of non-violent resistance to racial segregation. An ordained pastor in 1947, during his studies he came across the works of Gandhi, whose ideas became the core of his philosophy of non-violent protest. In 1954, he accepted the appointment as pastor of a Baptist church in Montgomery (Alabama). That same year, the U.S. Supreme Court ruled that racial segregation in state schools was illegitimate, and, pending that decision, segregation was challenged in all public places in the southern states. In 1955 King was in charge of the boycott of Montgomery's public transportation: the aim was to protest the arrest of Rosa Parks, the black woman who had refused to give her seat to a white passenger. During the protest, which lasted 381 days, King was arrested and imprisoned and was threatened with death several times. The boycott ended in 1956 with the Supreme Court ruling that racial segregation on public transport in the city was illegal.

Montgomery's boycott was a victory for the non-violent protest movement, and Luther King's prestige increased significantly. Having traveled to India in 1959, he understood more clearly the satyagraha, the principle of non-violent persuasion advocated by Gandhi, which King was determined to use as the main instrument of social protest. The following year he resigned his post in Montgomery to become pastor of the Baptist Church of Ebenezer, Atlanta. It allowed him to devote himself more actively to leading the nascent civil rights movement. At the same time, the black leadership, which had previously been limited to promoting causes and proposing reconciliation, was undergoing a profound transformation and calling for change "by every possible means." New leaders and more radical groups emerged, such as Malcolm X's Black Muslims and Black Power, carrying different ideologies and methods of fighting racism. However, King's prestige guaranteed that non-violence, although not universally accepted, remained the official method of resistance. In 1963, Luther King led an intense civil rights campaign in Birmingham, Alabama, and others throughout the South to demand the inclusion of blacks on electoral lists, the abolition of racial segregation, and the improvement of the quality of education and housing. On August 28, 1963, he led the historic march on Washington and delivered the famous speech "I have a dream." In front of 2,500,000 people of all races, Martin Luther King touched the heart of the nation, and millions of people took action. America watches the event on television, but the whole world learns about it through newspapers and magazines. Those who march in Washington want to emphasize that they firmly believe in democratic institutions and the ability of the legislature to enforce justice.

"I say to you today, my friends, so even though we face the difficulties of today and tomorrow, *I still have a dream [...] I dream that one day this nation will* rise up and live out the true meaning of its creed. *I have a dream that one day [...]* the sons of former slaves and the sons of former slave owners will be able to sit down together at the table of brotherhood. [...]. I have a dream that my four little children will one day live in a nation where they will not be judged by the color of their skin but by the content of their character, I have a dream today! [...]"* [1]

In 1964 he was awarded the Nobel Peace Prize. On April 4, 1968, he was assassinated in Memphis, Tennessee.

The Civil Rights Act of 1964

The line of thought of the Reverend Martin Luther King Junior now reaches everywhere. It is very much felt and shared throughout the nation; his belief in the value and effectiveness of passive resistance as a form of social protest pushes the majority of the black population to rebellion.

The Movement towards the emancipation of the black population was also supported by the then President, John Fitzgerald Kennedy. In April 1963, he asked Congress to enact laws that would guarantee citizens equal access to public and private services. He demanded facilities that discrimination in

---

[1] Copyright 1963. Martin Luther King, JR

hiring by federal companies and institutions would not be allowed, and that the Federal Government would not provide any financial support in programs or activities involving racial discrimination.

President Kennedy's June 19, 1963 message to the nation has not only historical value, but is a milestone on the United States' path to equality. In 1964, one year after his death, the Civil Rights Act became law. When President Kennedy was assassinated on November 22, 1963, many leaders of the black Movement feared that the path to equality and justice would come to a halt.

Despite this enthusiasm for justice and equality that runs throughout the nation, there are still considerable obstacles in all states, and at all levels to the process of desegregation; everything was proceeding at a languid pace, from the education sector to the employment sector, up to the banal and daily gesture of drinking coffee. It is made more bitter and challenging by the fact that, to a greater extent, more than whites, blacks live in extreme poverty; in a society where abundance and luxury prevail, blacks cannot find work, unlike their white peers. A large proportion of the black population receives social benefits and lives in ghettos in inhuman conditions, where crime is often the only possible activity.

Although violence is limited and marginal, however, dramatic events persist, such as murders and attacks not only against blacks but also against those whites who have made them fight discrimination. Organizations such as the Ku Klux Klan or the lesser-known White Citizens Councils exist and are still active.

PROTESTS CONTINUE

In the 1960s, the black protest movement also developed, thanks to the work of Martin Luther King.

The **Black Muslims**, a movement founded in the 1930s by Wallace Fard, claim to be initially children of Islam and to have Allah as their God. If, in the name of this religion, American blacks will unite and play an active role in it, they will be able to acquire lost power again. The Black Muslims, convinced that the leading cause of discrimination is due to the lack of economic power on the part of blacks, try to favor any activity on their own. In 1964, Malcolm X was the most significant leader of the Movement and the first to speak openly of the **Black Revolution**. In the same year, he detached himself from the Movement to found a collateral one called Organization of Afro-American Unity; not even a year later, he was assassinated. Although Malcolm X had a personality and professed a different political and religious belief from M.L.King, he remains a prominent figure in the Black Movement, thanks in part to his autobiography, which contributed significantly to making him famous after his death.

The Black Power and the Black Panther Party

The disappointment in white people's institutions and the eternal struggle against discrimination leads black Muslims to believe that the road to equality is definitively blocked for them. Hence the challenging attitudes towards the United States and its institutions. In 1966, with Stokely Carmichael, Black Power was founded.

In its most positive sense, Black Power wants to promote self-determination, self-respect, and full participation in decisions concerning blacks. Carmichael published in 1967, together with C.V. Hamilton, a book entitled Black Power, which is exposed to the lines of the policy that should lead to the "liberation" of black Americans. This Movement rejects the principles of non-violence and the integration of blacks into American society. These beliefs are the basis of the civil rights movement, of which M.L. King was the principal animator. However, it wants the use of violent means to be limited to the sole purpose of self-defense. The Movement incites blacks to fight for higher economic and political power by carefully using their ballot papers in both local and legislative elections, stimulates self-respect among black people, promotes black people's interest in their history and culture, and encourages them to rely on their own strengths and be proud of "Negritude." For Black Power,

71

blacks should seek to form independent political parties and build a coalition with poor whites in the South. The economic, social, and cultural organizations of black people should be led exclusively by black people. Thus, for example, in the school field, black parents should end the control of public schools in their communities by appointing teachers and choosing textbooks.

Carmichael argues that only the attainment of these ideals can force whites to deal with blacks. In reality, these associative groups will be involved by nationalist movements in the overthrow of the political, economic, and social system.

The best known and most widespread of these is the Black Panther Party, founded in 1966 in Oakland, California, by Bobby Seale and Huey P. Newton. Influenced by Marxism and the preaching of intellectuals like Malcolm X, the militants replaced the principle of non-violence preached by M.L. King with that of self-defense as an instrument of struggle against the object of a hard campaign of repression by the police and F.B.I.; all this resulted in a tight guerrilla war with the forces of law and order, until their crisis at the beginning of the Seventies.

The years '66, '67, and '68 saw many violent rebellions caused by living conditions in the ghettos: blacks want jobs, decent homes, and better schools. The assassination of Martin Luther King is not only a dramatic and regrettable historical event that seems to indicate the end of a non-violent rebellion, but showed, as in the case of the assassination of J.F.Kennedy and Senator Robert Kennedy, then-presidential candidate, how far men could go to prevent the realization of those ideals of justice and equality that are fundamental for a democratic society. In those same years, the Kerner investigation, financed by the government, reveals that the country is increasingly moving towards two distinct, separate, and unequal societies: that of whites and that of blacks. The Black Muslims and the Black Power do not want peaceful integration. Furthermore, the blacks have not found a valid alternative to violence as a means of achieving just ideals, and the resulting sense of frustration leads them to hostility towards institutions and government.

However, the process of desegregation continues unceasingly and with positive results. For 20 years (from the 1950s to the 1970s) many things have changed for black people, the Civil Rights Act has set irremovable benchmarks for the fight against equality and equal opportunities.

CHAPTER 7: THE CLOSED FIST

On October 16, 1968, in the Olympic Stadium in Mexico City, U.S. sprinters Tommie Smith and John Carlos came first and third in the 200-meter final. Smith had set a new world record, with 19.83 seconds, despite having an injured tendon and having run the last 10 meters by raising his arms. Carlos, with his 20.10 seconds, had arrived behind Australian Peter Norman, who, with his 20.06 seconds, had finished second.

After Smith and Carlos received their medals on the podium for the award ceremony, they turned towards the huge U.S. flag hanging above the stands and waited for the start of the anthem. When the notes of *The Star-Spangled Banner* resonated in the stadium, Smith and Carlos lowered their heads and raised a closed fist, wearing black gloves to protest against racial discrimination in the U.S. Their gesture, with their heads down during the American anthem, fully represents the politics that break into the sport, their support for the Black Panther Party, their support for an uprising that still marks American history today. But in reality, the arrogance of that "gesture of challenge," made with that bent head, is a gesture of suffering, melancholy, which eliminates the attitude of challenge. It becomes a tribute to the persecuted, the arrested, the murdered. To this day, it remains a historical moment of meaningful communication.

What about Norman, the foreign-looking white man? His story, less well known but just as worthy of remembrance. He fully supported the silent protest of two African-Americans. He asked to be allowed to wear a human rights badge at the ceremony, and he was totally on the right side.

Dozens of yards away, photographer John Dominis took a picture of them that would become one of the most famous of the 20th century, symbolizing a decade of black civil rights protests. The influence of Smith and Carlos' gesture can still be felt today: an example is the case of the African-American football players kneeling during the American anthem.

Behind Smith and Carlos's closed fist was the battle for civil rights, and in particular, for those of African Americans, which had reached its peak in 1968. In subsequent interviews, Smith explained that his and Carlos' was not the greeting of Black Power, the slogan of the African American protests, but more generally a gesture of protest in favor of human rights. The two athletes chose different symbolic devices to participate in the award ceremony. They went barefoot and wearing black stockings to represent the poverty of African Americans. Smith wore a black scarf, while Carlos unbuttoned his suit to show solidarity with the American workers. He wore a pearl necklace to symbolize the stones used in the lynchings of African Americans. But Carlos forgot his gloves that day, so Smith lent him one: that's why they raised different arms. Their protest was discreetly joined by the athlete who came second, Norman, who wore an OPHR brooch.

During the award ceremony, silence fell on the stadium. The International Olympic Committee (I.O.C.) immediately demanded the exclusion of Smith and Carlos from the Olympic village and their suspension from the American team for having made a political event at the Olympics. At first, the U.S. Olympic Committee refused but had to adapt in the face of pressure from the I.O.C.

On their return to the United States, Smith and Carlos suffered extensive criticism and received threats and intimidation. They became heroes for the African-American community, however, and in the following decades, they won awards and recognition for their protest. After the Olympics, both had careers in the N.F.L., the professional football league, and then as athletic coaches.

Norman also received insults and threats back in Australia. According to some people, he was excluded from the 1972 Olympics because of the protest. Years later, in 2006, when Norman died of a heart attack, Smith and Carlos carried his coffin to his funeral.

CHAPTER 8: THE RIOTS

1) Harlem, 1935

The story would seem trivial, were it not for the fact that this, for historians, is the first modern racial uprising in the U.S.A. It all begins on the afternoon of March 19, when a clerk from the Kress Five and Ten department store, in front of the Apollo Theatre on 125th Street, stops a 12-year-old black boy of Puerto Rican origin: Lino Ravera. He is caught stealing a pocket knife worth 10 cents on the dollar. The man threatens to take Lino to the dungeon and beat the shit out of him if he sees him in the shop again. The boy then bites his hand, and the other salesmen call the police. A small crowd gathers to see what's happening. A woman starts screaming that the boy has been beaten. She thinks so because she sees the blood on the clerk's hand, the one that came out after Lino's bite. From that moment on, word spreads in the neighborhood that a black kid was beaten to death. In the evening, a group of young people demonstrates in front of the Kress Five and Ten store. That was the first damage, which will then spread to all white people's shops in the area. Law enforcement officials intervened. The riot will die down the next day. There were three dead, dozens injured, and millions of dollars worth of damage. Mayor Fiorello La Guardia was forced to spread photos showing Lino Ravera, alive and well, to convince the rebels that he was not dead. La Guardia also set up a commission to understand the reasons for the rebellion.

Injustice, racial discrimination in the workplace and by the police, were the reasons that emerged.

2) Philadelphia, 1964

It stems from a road dispute. In the summer of that year, the tension is sky-high in the city. All the rounds of the African-American community denounce acts of abuse of power by white cops and anger mounts. Following its policy of "consensus and sympathy," the Police Department decides to send mixed patrols to the black majority neighborhoods. A black cop will flank a white one, just to make it clear that there are no distinctions. On August 28, two officers Robert Wells (black) and John Hoff (white), find themselves in front of Odessa Bradford, a black woman who is stuck in her car in a traffic jam on Columbia Avenue. The first offer of help turns into an argument when the woman refuses to get out of her car, and the fuse that will set off the fire will be there when the two policemen try to force her out of the vehicle. Word is spreading that two officers beat up a pregnant black woman. At night, there are dozens of white store fires. By a miracle, there will be no deaths, but more than 300 injured and almost 700 arrests.

3) Watts, 1965

For a week, this suburb of Los Angeles was burned to the ground. The most violent and bloody revolt, second only to the one that broke out almost thirty years later, in the same Californian city. The spark, also, in this case, was a police check on a black man accused of driving under the influence of drugs, which soon turned into a physical confrontation with the officers. A woman was involved, and again the flames were fuelled by rumors that a pregnant young black woman had been brutally beaten by the police. Watts was one of the few areas where blacks were allowed to live, and for some time, the local community had been complaining about the police aggressive policy towards African American teenagers. To stop the uprising, the National Guard had to intervene. Almost 6,000 soldiers and police officers faced the anger of 35,000 people. From August 11 to 17, there were 34 dead, more than a thousand wounded, more than three thousand arrests, and 40 million dollars worth of damage. Also, in this case, there was an investigation into the social causes of the revolt. The results were a photocopy of those produced in 1935 by the commission that emerged after the Harlem revolt: racial segregation, poverty, injustices were the basis of Watts' summer of blood.

4) Detroit, 1967

With its 43 dead (a dozen white people, the rest black), the Detroit riot is in third place in the particular ranking of bloody pin riots in U.S. history, after New York during the Civil War and after Los Angeles in 1992. In those years, even though the federal government had spent many millions of dollars to fund the social programs of Lyndon Johnson's Great Society, and despite the emergence of a black middle class in the city over the years, who were sometimes wealthy and open to the professions, most of the African-American population of Detroit lived in poverty and social exclusion. Frustration was at a very high level. It exploded when the police raided an unlicensed club where about 80 people were celebrating the return of two veterans from Vietnam. All participants in the party (the vast majority of black) were arrested. The crowd that had gathered outside the building started throwing bottles at the police cars. From 23 to July 27, the city was at the mercy of the violence. The governor of Michigan, George Romney (Mitt's father, who is also a Republican candidate for the White House), called in the National Guard: President Lydon Johnson sent in the army. In addition to dozens of deaths, the uprising caused nearly 2000 injuries, more than 7000 arrests, and the destruction of 2000 buildings. The economic losses were enormous. Many investors left the city and never returned.

5) After the death of Martin Luther King, 1968
The Mayor of New York, John Lindsay, immediately went to Harlem to give his solidarity to the African American community. Robert Kennedy gave a speech in Indianapolis, James Brown sang at his concert in Boston. These three facts prevented the uprising from spreading to these three cities after the news that Martin Luther King had been killed had been spread on April 4. But this was not the case in dozens of other American cities. The black people expressed their anger at the

assassination of the civil rights campaigner. The violence continued for four or five days, from the East Coast to the West Coast. There were numerous deaths, and dozens were injured. The army and the Civil Guard were deployed in Washington, Kansas City, Baltimore, Chicago. Jeeps and armored cars were on the streets. America looked like a country at war. President Lyndon Johnson said he wasn't surprised by that explosion of violence. It helped hasten the passage of the Civil Rights Act.

6) The Kitty Hawk black people's revolt, 1972

It happened as a veritable mutiny on racial grounds. Two hundred black sailors of the U.S.S. Kitty Hawk, one of the prestigious aircraft carriers of the American navy, that night of October 11, 1972, rebelled against their officers, who was accused of wanting to impose an openly racist regime on the boat. The ship was off the coast of Vietnam, engaged in a war operation, but for the insurgents, the enemies were on board. There were violent brawls for hours and hours between white sailors and black sailors. The commander of the carrier managed to persuade them to return to their posts a few hours before the war operation to which the ship had been assigned began. The news of the uprising was reported in the New York Times. Some sailors were later court-martialed.

7) Miami, 1980

A police patrol chases a black motorist, stopped him, and control turns into a collision. The man was beaten and died from his wounds. No one will be able to stop the anger of the people. He was 33 years old Arthur McDuffie, when he was killed. A few months later, the court decided there were no guilty officers. Outside the courtroom, 5000 people were waiting for justice. When acquittal came, the riot broke out. It started in Overtown and then moved to downtown Miami. In the first few hours, there were three victims. The next day, there were 12 dead. The National Guard arrived, and a curfew was imposed. A state of emergency was declared in the city.

8) Los Angeles, 1992

The hidden social tensions of the eighties exploded in the second year of the new decade in California when a court found the police officers who had stopped and beaten Rodney King, a motorist, not guilty. For six days, the city of California was the scene of clashes and violence. Local and national television picked up live coverage of the scenes from hell's day.

A truck driver Reginald Denny was driving down Florence Avenue in Los Angeles to a factory in the Inglewood neighborhood. Denny, a 36-year-old white, did not have a car radio on his truck and did not know anything about what had been happening in the South Los Angeles area for a few hours. Hundreds of people, mostly African-American, were ravaging the streets and carrying out looting and summary violence in protest of a court decision to acquit four police officers who had brutally beaten a black motorist. It was just seven o'clock in the evening, and Denny was crossing Normandie Avenue when people threw rocks through his windshield and yelled at him to stop. He did, and two African-American men pulled him out of the car before they kicked and hammered him. Denny tried to get up, but one of the two men hit him in the head with a piece of brick, fracturing his skull in 97 places and leaving him unconscious on the ground. Then he laughed and did a kind of dance, making gangster gestures facing the helicopter cameras that were filming the scene. The two men stole his wallet and spit on him; another stole a bag from his truck, and another kicked Denny when he tried to get up. Two African-American men and two women who lived nearby, Bobby Green, Lei Yuille, Titus Murphy, and Terri Barnett, were watching television at home when they saw what was happening to Denny. They got out and rushed to the intersection of Florence and Normandie: when they arrived, they helped Denny into the truck and drove him to a hospital in Inglewood. In addition to his skull fractures, Denny had suffered brain damage, and an eye had dislocated from his orbit, but he managed to save himself. The attack on Reginald Denny had a considerable media impact because it happened live on television: it became the symbol of the 1992 Los Angeles riots, one of the most dramatic and incredible events in recent American history, in which 63 people died, more than two thousand were injured, more than 11 thousand were arrested, and more than a billion dollars worth of damage was caused.

9) Saint Petersburg, 1997

There was a police check and a dead motorist. The script is always the same. But, the tragic lesson five years earlier, perhaps, had been learned. The impact of the violence was less, the reaction also. Young African Americans demonstrate all night, throwing bottles at police cars. A few gunshots were also fired, but no one was seriously injured, and no one lost their head. The riot ended after a few hours.

10) Cincinnati, 2001

The statistics were clear: between 1995 and 2001, at least fifteen black men under 40 had died while in police custody. There was already an emotional climate in the city due to a couple of trials involving similar cases when the news of the death of Timothy Thomas, a young man who the police had stopped at least a dozen times in the last year, came to light. The final check had been fatal. The officer later explained that he reacted to what appeared to him to be an aggressive move by the boy. The next day, Timothy's mother and a couple of hundred people interrupted the city council in protest. On the street, there were already protest demonstrations. And when the cops were ordered to disperse them with tear gas, the riot officially began. Since then and throughout the night, looting and damage alternated with attacks on police patrols. The incidents went on for three nights and only ended when a curfew was imposed

CHAPTER 9: BROKEN YOUNG LIVES

Trayvon Martin, 2012

When security guard George Zimmerman, responsible for the death of 17-year-old African-American Trayvon Martin, was found not guilty, the anger of the black community was unleashed.

Protest marches began throughout the United States. There were online campaigns, in which public figures and thousands of Facebook and Twitter users wore hoodies. A police chief and a magistrate were forced to quit their jobs in Florida to try to quell protests and tensions. Once again, it was a story of ethnic prejudice, and of racism, which runs like a known, but destabilizing fever in American society. For him, even Barack Obama took to the field, where he spoke out for the feelings of the black people of America and made a statement that a president of the United States other than himself could never have said. He said: *"If I had a son, he'd look like Trayvon."*

Trayvon had spent the afternoon at his girl's father's house in a Sanford suburb of Orlando. During a break from the basketball game on T.V., the boy decided to go shopping for candy at a nearby 7 Eleven store. On the way home, he meets George Zimmerman, a volunteer vigilante from the area who, suspicious of the boy (wearing a hoodie), starts following him. An argument soon breaks out between the two of them. Zimmerman calls 911 and tells the operator (who advises him not to intervene) that "this guy looks shady, is drugged or something similar." During the altercation, Trayvon also calls a friend (who later testifies that he overheard Zimmerman making racist insults like "fucking nigger"). The quarrel soon degenerates into a confrontation. Some locals say they heard Trayvon screaming, calling for help. Then, the gunshot. The police arrive a few minutes later, and saw the boy lying on the ground, lifeless.

During the interrogation following the shooting, Zimmerman, a 28-year-old Hispanic man, said he acted in self-defense. He felt threatened behind the boy's back as he got back into his car after the altercation. However, the investigation showed that Trayvon Martin was unarmed and that he did not carry any objects that might pose a threat (when he was found dead by the police, he had a plastic bag with candy and iced tea next to him). The Orlando police did not arrest Zimmerman based on a Florida law allowing the use of "lethal weapons" in self-defense. "He had no criminal record whatsoever," explained Sanford Police Chief Bill Lee.

"We want to see Zimmerman in the courtroom with his hands tied behind his back, indicted for the death of a boy, Trayvon Martin!", shouted the hundreds and hundreds of people who participated in one of the many protest demonstrations in Orlando, with the boy's father and mother (another, equally massive, was organized in Union Square, New York). The story

grew, becoming for many, especially in the African-American community, a new emblem of injustice and prejudice. First, the behavior of the local police and judiciary was questioned. It is not true that Zimmerman had no precedent. In the past, he had been fighting with a police officer and had been reported by his ex-girlfriend for domestic violence. It is not even clear if he had warned the Twin Lakes owners' association, the gated community that he was in charge of, of his being armed. Some people in the neighborhood describe him as being mainly motivated by racial hatred. "He came by our house, and warned us against young black people seen wandering around the neighborhood," they said.

In an attempt to alleviate controversy and accusations, eventually, Bill Lee, Sanford's chief of police, and the county prosecutor, Norman Wolfinger, decided to take a step back and drop the case. The Governor of Florida, Rick Scott nominated a new prosecutor and created a commission of inquiry into the matter, which will be led by his deputy, Jennifer Carroll (who is African-American). Meanwhile, the F.B.I. And the U.S. Department of Justice have announced their own independent investigations, and Change.org, a site that promotes social justice cases through online petitions, has collected more than a million signatures for the arrest of Zimmerman (who, joined by dozens of death threats, left his apartment and he was lost track of. Under indictment was the behavior of the Florida police and judiciary, as well as the state's self-defense law (which allows you to shoot, for self-defense purposes, without even trying to step back a few steps before pulling the trigger). Under indictment, however, is an entire system made up of culture, perceptions, prejudices rooted in history, and the depths of American society. But, would he have been killed, if Trayvon Martin, wasn't a black teenager in a hood?

Michael Brown, 2014

The country had to deal with another case of an unarmed young African American. This time, in Ferguson, Texas.

Hundreds of people gathered on August 10, 2014, to remember Michael Brown, the 18-year-old shot by Officer Darren Wilson the night before. The boy had been stopped by the St. Louis police officer on his way home with a friend.

The wake turned into a series of looting and clashes with police that lasted all night.

A small group of participants broke away from the main event and attacked some shops overlooking the street where Brown was killed. Local TV footage showed dozens of people entering through the smashed windows of some boutiques, liquor, and cell phone stores, and coming out with boxes and other looted material. Other people attacked police cars and those parked along the street. A television van was also attacked.

According to the journalists present, the police tried above all to contain the protest and prevent other people from reaching the looting site, rather than confront the people involved in the looting themselves. The clashes seem to have ended overnight and without injuries, but there have been unconfirmed reports of incidents during the morning as well. The police said that only a small group of people took part in the looting.

The killing of Brown has been associated by many with that of Trayvon Martin, a 17-year-old boy killed by the vigilante in February 2012. Martin, like Brown, was also unarmed. He was shot six times; two to the head.

Darren Wilson, the 28-year-old policeman, claimed that Martin had attacked him, that he was angry as hell. Eyewitnesses said; however, he didn't react to the arrest.

Five hundred pages of transcripts were produced and published by the St. Louis County Attorney General[2]. They compared the witnesses' statements with those of the police officer. Based on these testimonies and documentary evidence, the grand jury determined that Officer Wilson did not commit any crime and that he did not act outside the law in killing Michael Brown.

Subsequently, the FBI and the Department of Justice opened two files to investigate allegations of further racial discrimination and abuse of force by the Ferguson Police Department.

CHAPTER 10: POLICE BRUTALITY

A country with the highest incarceration rate in the world, the U.S. is generally a state with an historically endemic social deviance. Traditionally considered to be exclusively related to the criminal world; in reality, this deviance is a characteristic that can also be found in the behavior of the police corps: we are talking about police brutality.

U.S. law enforcement, traditionally known as an apparatus with extremely repressive tendencies, especially for a democratic nation, has a history stained by countless cases of physical and psychological violence, corruption, abuse of power, perpetrated against American citizens. Much of this violence is directed against African American and Hispanic communities in the country, in line with the cultural trends of a society that is still deeply divided by the racial issue and where minorities are subject to harsh discrimination.

In the U.S.A., where deep racial inequalities between blacks and whites persist today, one of the most critical factors in their reproduction is determined precisely by police behavior. Exploiting their authority, which is supported by a Constitution that has progressively broadened the legitimacy of their abusive actions and the historical bipartisan political will to use the hard fist against criminals or alleged criminals, the police corps has always been a fundamental agent in the process of marginalization, criminalization and violent repression of black communities, since the times of Reconstruction. There are three essential knots in the matter. The first is why the American police force is so violent, and why this violence is directed primarily against African Americans and Hispanics. The second concerns the destructive consequences of this phenomenon in the relationships of trust between citizens and institutions. The third, finally, is about the most effective policies for reducing police brutality.

The reason for police brutality: the cultural factor and the social context

In considering why American law enforcement agencies make such diligent use of violent methods, the most crucial factor to consider is cultural. Police brutality seems to be conveyed above all through an extraordinarily corporatist and silent internal culture, which exalts the machismo of the agents, promotes sharper and harsher solutions, and is permeated with profound and radical racism. Police officers have, historically, moved in a social context where the cataloging of specific fragments of society (in this case, racial minorities) has met with the approval of a good part of the institutions and civil society. During slavery and Reconstruction, the police often worked to repress the ambitions of those Afro-Americans who sought emancipation. The same happened during Jim Crow's segregationism, where police repression of civil rights activists clashed with their permissive and lax attitude towards whites who committed real acts of terrorism against African Americans. Finally, the police were the institution that, in recent decades, more than any other, has contributed to the increase in the incarceration rates of blacks and Latinos, locking millions of individuals in U.S. prisons. In such a profoundly racist social context, police brutality thrives when officers are allowed to use a destructive force against minorities, who are already the most fragile and marginalized part of society. The discriminatory culture that permeates American community is also conveyed through the action of the police, who, by absorbing the values of the context of which they are part, become an agent in the process of reproducing racial inequalities. Thus, the use of violent methods becomes instrumental in maintaining an order that goes beyond the legal one, touching the nerve of the racial issue.

The social divide between law enforcement and the black community

The scale of the phenomenon is considerable. Between 2017 and 2018, the American police committed 2,311 murders, representing more than three per day. The murder rate of African Americans is three times higher than that of whites. Of the victims of color (blacks and Latinos), almost 40% were killed while unarmed; among whites, only 14%. But the most disconcerting thing is that the vast majority of cases do not result in investigations, suspensions, or convictions in court of agents. The system protects them, making it impossible for U.S.

law enforcement agencies to take responsibility for their conduct and thus act undisturbed. The War on Drugs and mass imprisonment, with the targeting of black communities and the escalation of violence, abuse of power, and arrests, are only the last piece in a long and consistent historical process. The police arrest blacks and Latinos at a disproportionate rate compared to whites, although there is no difference in the rate of crimes committed. Recent incidents, such as that of some NYPD officers who reported a superior officer who ordered them to "stop more blacks and Latinos," are the litmus test of a climate poisoned by deep-rooted racial discrimination.

In such a context, where violence is widespread, where it is mostly racially motivated, and where there are no mechanisms for empowering agents, the relationship between law enforcement and minorities has deteriorated. Already characterized by a healthy distrust of institutions, accused of leaving their neighborhoods in a state of neglect, these communities suffer a relationship with the police that inspires fear and evokes deep social trauma, instead of creating security.

Conclusions and policy

Reflecting on the society in which they operate, the American police seem to have assimilated many of the cultural trends inherent in the context in which they operate, and has become an extremely violent and repressive body. The rootedness of racism in the U.S. translates into law enforcement agencies with markedly discriminatory tendencies, which contributes to giving much of the violence a racial connotation. Finally, corporatism and the absence of accountability mechanisms for agents who commit abuses of power create a protective shield, which makes it difficult to impose sanctions on police departments that can reduce violent behavior.

Nevertheless, there are virtuous cases in the U.S., and the effect of specific policies that have a proven result in reducing violence by law enforcement agencies. In particular, restricting the use of certain methods of intervention such as chokeholds, imposing of greater transparency on agents when compiling reports, clearly defining if and when violent methods can be used, working on de-escalation and imposing the use of firearms only as a last resort, are some of the most effective measures.

Some departments have already implemented some of these solutions. By adopting them, the level of violence committed against citizens has decreased. Not only that: the use of these techniques also benefits the agents, and reduces the probability that they will be killed or injured in the field. They are, in essence, solutions that create greater security for both citizens and the police.

It is clear, however, that a cultural change within the departments is also necessary. The reduction of violence by police officers in the U.S. also depends on their willingness to be more transparent in their conduct and on how hard they will work to eliminate the racial bias that has historically influenced their course of action.

CHAPTER 11: THE BEST FILMS ABOUT THE FIGHT FOR CIVIL RIGHTS

Many of the chapters we read in this book have also been told through the movies. The cinema narrated the most critical episodes of the struggle for civil rights undertaken by the African-American population in the South of the United States. Watching some films about that period of conflicts and conquests, achieved with thanks to the protest movement led by Martin Luther King and other significant charismatic figures, can be the ideal way to prepare for a tour through the struggle for the affirmation of Civil Rights, and earning a preliminary geographical and historical awareness to get excited and moved even before you leave.

Below we present a guide to the most notable films on white racism and black claims in those 1950s and 1960s that, from the deep rural province of America, have changed and made the world fairer.

To Kill a Mockingbird (1962)

To Kill a Mockingbird (published in 1960) is a cinematic transposition of Harper Lee's masterpiece. The writer drew inspiration from the racist and segregationist society of his native village, Monroeville, Alabama. The film faithfully follows the story of the novel, focusing on the defense lawyer Atticus Finch agreeing to take on the black Tom Robinson, falsely accused by a drunk farmer of sexual violence against his daughter. Although proved innocent during the trial, Robinson will end up a victim of fanatical white intolerance. The figure of Finch, played by Gregory Peck, won first place in the American

Film Institute's particular ranking of heroes of American cinema in 2003.

In the Heat of the Night *(1967)*

Based on John Ball's novel "In the Heat of the Night" (1965), this detective story with a strong social connotation, released the year before Martin Luther King's murder, is set in the deep Mississippi. The black Inspector Virgil Tibs (Sidney Poitier), of the Philadelphia homicide squad, is solving a case involving the prejudices that weigh on the African-American population. Despite initial mistrust, a relationship of mutual esteem is finally established with local police officer Bill Gillespie (Rod Steiger).

Mississippi Burning (1988)

The film is inspired by a historical episode, the murder of three Mississippi civil rights activists on the night of June 21-22, 1964: James Earl Chaney, Andrew Goodman, Michael Schwerner (the last two are white people).

There is an FBI investigation, promoted by the Federal Government despite opposition from the state government, called Mississippi Burning. Agents Rupert Anderson and Alan Ward (Gene Hackman and Willem Dafoe) can identify 18 members of a Neshoba County Klu Klux Klan fringe as the culprits, while also ascertaining the complicity of the local sheriff. The shooting took place mainly in Jackson County, Vicksburg, and Vaiden (Mississippi) and LaFayette (Alabama). In Neshoba County, the Zion Methodist Church, which was the object of an intimidating fire at the time, the local prison and court, and theatres of events, are part of a Historic District included in the US Civil Rights Trail.

The Long Walk Home (1990)

The storyline, located in Alabama, narrates the boycott of public transport in Montgomery, which took place after the arrest of Rosa Parks (1955), and was coordinated by Martin Luther King. The story is seen through two female figures, Odessa (Whoopi Golberg), a black babysitter, and her employer (Miriam), who develop strong solidarity in the face of a racist and masculine society. The capital of Alabama is one of the essential goals on the US Civil Rights Trail, with the remarkable Rosa Parks Museum.

Malcolm X (1992)

This film is based on the autobiography of Malcolm X, written with Alex Haley, who also collaborated on the screenplay. It is a colossal film in which Denzel Washington admirably plays the Islamic faith activist, born in Omaha, Nebraska, and murdered in New York at the age of 39.

Ghosts of Mississippi (1996)

On the night of June 12, 1963, a mysterious gunshot killed Medgar Evers, civil rights activist and secretary of the National Association for the Advancement of Black People in Mississippi. He is accused of the murder of Byron De La Beckwith, a supporter of white supremacy, but after two trials, he is released, and the episode seems to end there. Thirty years later, Bobby Delaughter, assistant district attorney, manages to reopen the case, helped by the widow Myrlie. Bobby risks compromising his marriage, interrupting a brilliant career, and endangering his wife and children, but with great courage, he goes ahead.

The Help (2011)

Skeeter, a white girl, and a new college graduate, decided to go home to her wealthy parents in Mississippi. The girl wants to become a writer and starts working in a small local newspaper, where she is in charge of answering housewives' mail. The hypocrisy and racism prevailing in the sixties led her to collect in a book, the point of view of the many African-American women who work as maids in white families, causing a scandal.

The Butler (2013)

After escaping from the segregationist tyranny of the South, the young Cecil Gaines devoted himself to a wide variety of tasks in order to learn qualities that could guarantee him a better future. The turning point came when Cecil got a job as a butler in the White House. Here Cecil bears direct witness to American history and intimately follows all the internal dynamics of the Oval Office during the years of the civil rights movement. The work allows Cecil to guarantee his family a comfortable life. Still, conflicts are not lacking and they emerge above all when the man's total devotion to the presidents creates a sharp contrast with Gloria and her son Louis, causing them both to leave. Meanwhile, America is marked by numerous events: from the assassination of John F. Kennedy and Martin Luther King to the Freedom Riders and Black Panther movements, and from the Vietnam War to the Watergate scandal.

Selma (2014)

1964 is the year that Martin Luther King Jr. receives the Nobel Peace Prize, and three black girls are killed by a bomb planted by the Ku Klux Klan in a Baptist church in Birmingham, Alabama. Annie Lee Cooper tries to register to vote in Selma but is prevented. When the pastor meets with the president of the United States to ask for federal action to allow African-American citizens to vote undisturbed, Lyndon B. Johnson tells him he has other priorities. Thus began King's campaign for the right to vote, culminating in the historic march from Selma to Montgomery in 1965.

Loving (2016)

Loving is a 2016 drama film written and directed by Jeff Nichols. It tells the true story of the Loving couple, protagonists of the famous "Loving vs. Virginia" lawsuit that led the Supreme Court to overturn the laws prohibiting interracial marriage in the United States. Central Point, Virginia, 1958. Richard Loving (Joel Edgerton), a white construction worker, and Mildred Jeter (Ruth Negga), a black girl, grew up together and are so in love that they want to build a family. When Mildred gets pregnant, they get married in Washington, DC, because in their state, interracial marriages are prohibited by law and severely punished.

Back home, they are arrested and sentenced to one year in prison. The spouses get a suspended sentence on the condition that they do not return to Virginia for 25 years, or at least not together. Five years later, they live in Washington, DC, with their three children, but they wish to return to the people they love in their land. One day, Mildred watches on TV the march on Washington for civil rights. Conquered by Martin Luther King's speech, she wrote a letter to Senator Robert Kennedy, asking him for help. The Lovings' case thus reaches the lawyer Bernie Cohen (Nick Kroll) of the American Union for Civil Liberties, who promises to help them to the end. Life magazine is also handling their case, giving it excellent media coverage. Thus begins the lawsuit that will lead them to change the Constitution of the United States.

All the Way (2016)

Steven Spielberg produces the film dedicated to the President of the United States Lyndon B. Johnson, and played by Bryan Cranston ("Breaking Bad"). The film tells the background of the first tumultuous year at the White House of the man who became President after the murder of John Fitzgerald Kennedy. As vice president, he swore on the plane that brought JFK's body back from Dallas and spent 11 months in the White House trying to get the Civil Rights Act passed by Kennedy and preparing the election campaign until the November 1964 elections.

CHAPTER 12: I CAN'T BREATHE

"I can't breathe" are the harrowing words George Floyd said before he died, as he was crushed by a police officer pressing his knee on his neck mercilessly.

They have now become the Black Lives Matter movement's cry of protest against police brutality.

George Floyd remained 8 minutes and 46 seconds with his face pressed firmly against the sidewalk, while the police officer's knee pressed against his neck. He stood there 8 minutes and 46 seconds, asking for help, begging, "Please, friend, please, I can't breathe." Then silence. But the knee of the caller 'friend' continued to press on his neck for another 3 minutes, despite the man on the ground no longer showing signs of life.

It is what happened on the evening of May 25, 2020, at the intersection of East 38th Street and Chicago Avenue in Minneapolis, Minnesota. These are the facts, documented by dozens of videos circulated on the web that has outraged the entire world. It is what led to the death of George Floyd and a series of epochal racial claims that are setting the streets of over 40 American cities, as well as numerous cities around the world on fire, to the cry of the slogan "I can't breathe," the last words uttered by the victim.

On the evening of Monday 25 May, George Floyd, a 46-year-old African-American, goes to buy a pack of cigarettes in the Cup Foods store where he is a regular customer. At the checkout that evening, however, there is one Mike Abumayyaleh, an employee of the shop. Still a young employee who, believing the $20 bill tendered by Floyd to be fake, calls 911, the police emergency services. At 8:08 p.m., Thomas K. Lane and J. Alexander Kueng of the Minneapolis Police Department (Mpd) arrive on the scene. After a brief interview with the employee on duty, they head towards the blue Suv parked on the opposite side of the street, where Floyd is sitting with two other people. Agent Lane pulls out his gun and orders Floyd to put his hands on the steering wheel, then drags him out of his car and handcuffs him, informing him that he is under arrest for using counterfeit money.

According to the reconstruction of the facts, also made possible by the mobile phone footage of the people attending the scene, George Floyd tries to clear his name and, although already handcuffed, puts up a mild resistance when officers try to get him behind the wheel of the police car. At 8.12 p.m., Kueng blocks Floyd, still handcuffed, on the sidewalk against the wall in front of the Dragon Wok restaurant.

According to local prosecutors, the man is said to be claustrophobic and unable to breathe. At 8.17 p.m., police officers Derek Michael Chauvin and Tou Thao arrive as reinforcements to the officers present on the scene, trying to load Floyd onto the steering wheel by moving him from the driver's side to the passenger side.

More and more people start filming the scene that is consumed before their eyes: at 8.19 p.m. Chauvin drags Floyd out of his car, making him fall face down on the sidewalk still handcuffed. At 8:20 p.m., a driver stopped at the Speedway LLC gas station starts filming the scene: Floyd is on the ground beside the curb, and Officer Chauvin presses his knee on the handcuffed man's neck while officers Kueng and Lane put pressure on his torso and legs.

In the video, you can hear the man distinctly say, "Please, I can't breathe" and "Please, please, please, please." Other people also start filming what is happening and ask the officers to help the arrested man by reporting that he has a nosebleed. Only at 8.22 p.m. the policemen call the ambulance declaring first a 'codice two', not an emergency, and then they request the intervention for a 'codice three', that is an emergency.

Officer Chauvin continues to press his knee on Floyd's neck despite the man's calls for help and the many witnesses calling for help. At 8.25 p.m. George Floyd appears unconscious, but Chauvin will only lift his knee after the paramedics call for help, regardless of the fact that the man has been unconscious for over 3 minutes. He was clinically declared dead at Hennepin County Medical Center in Minneapolis.

According to the Hennepin Medical Center's autopsy, released on May 30, Floyd's body showed no signs of asphyxiation or strangulation that could have been fatal, but previous medical conditions, such as heart hypertension and coronary artery disease, which may have been aggravated by Officer Chauvin's maneuver. On June 1, the results of the autopsy commissioned by the family and performed by Dr. Michael Baden of the University of Michigan and Dr. Allecia Wilson were released. According to this autopsy, George Floyd died of "asphyxia caused by compression of the neck and back." A result that contrasts sharply with the statement in the official autopsy that "the combined effects of being blocked by the police, his past illnesses and some potential intoxicating substance in his body contributed to his death."

Derek Chauvin and the other three officers involved were fired and charged with several charges. In particular, Derek Chauvin was indicted first for third-degree murder, i.e., when a particularly cruel act is perpetrated without intent to kill, and then for second-degree manslaughter, when "a person knowingly risks causing death or serious physical harm to another." Finally, the incrimination for the agent has been changed to voluntary homicide, thanks to the intense anger of civil society. It turned out that Derek Chauvin, a Minneapolis

Police Department officer since 2001, already had 18 complaints against him for violence committed during the police service at the time of the murder.

The tension for the umpteenth racially motivated murder has reached the highest levels, transforming, in many cases, such demonstrations from peaceful to violent. The police intervened by shooting tear gas and rubber bullets into the crowd while the police station was set on fire and shops and police cars were vandalized. A CNN journalist Omar Jimenez, also an African-American, was arrested in New York City while conducting a live broadcast of the clashes in the streets. The images of the demonstrations in Minneapolis went around the world, involving more than 40 American cities in a single motion of anger. The death of George Floyd has reopened the national debate on the abuses perpetrated by many members of the police forces against the African-American population. According to recent estimates, this represents 20% of the people of Minneapolis. Still, as many as 60% of the victims of the shootings of the local police is represented, in the last ten years, by black people. The wave of protests, which started from the city where the event took place, has spread rapidly throughout the country, following the demonstrations carried out by the movement 'Black Lives Matter, born in 2016 to denounce and put a stop to racism, violence, and abuse of power of the forces of order against African Americans.

In many cities, already recovering from the lockdown due to the Covid-19 pandemic, a curfew has been imposed since 8 p.m. But in New York, people continue to take to the streets to demonstrate, violating this order. The chorus of protest has spread around the globe, involving authorities all over the world.

From the U.S. to Europe and beyond, there is a part of the world that kneels to remember him; that populates the squares and streets to protest against the circumstances in which his life was turned off; that repeats "George Floyd" because "silence=death;" that wears t-shirts and raises signs that say "I can't breathe." The mourning also passes through social channels and assumes proportions probably never seen before.

While Twitter flags and hides Trump's tweet that "glorified violence (Trump tweeted "When the looting starts, the shooting starts," referring to protests), **Queen Elizabeth** joins the protest through her organization "The Queen's Commonwealth Trust," which launches a tweet with explicit content: "Silence is not an option."[3]

Even the Duchess of Sussex, **Meghan Markle** says, "George Floyd's life mattered." And to the young people, "I'm sorry you have to grow up in a world like this."

---

[3] https://twitter.com/queenscomtrust/status/1267430722157056001

From his living room in Washington, DC, live on Zoom, the first African-American president in history, **Barack Obama**, spoke on the events surrounding the death of George Floyd. The footage was aired on all CNN channels, YouTube, and other stations. "I've never seen a crisis this severe in my life. We need to use it to provoke a nationwide awakening." A speech awaited by many in these days of angry protests around the United States. The former US President defends and claims the demonstrations in the streets, referring to America's history.

The speech was held a few hours after the Minneapolis prosecutor's office aggravated the indictment of the accused cop for Floyd's death: the charge became voluntary manslaughter.

In seeing what is happening, he says he is encouraged by the many young people he saw taking to the streets. He sees in them "a new mentality." Obama speaks to the millions of Americans who have taken to the streets and made their voices heard in a wave of protests born of legitimate frustration. To make a breakthrough, the role of activism will be crucial: for too long, America has failed to reform the methods of police and criminal justice.

To the peaceful protesters, the overwhelming majority, Obama offers his support, and calls them courageous, responsible, and capable of inspiring us, while condemning those who seek confrontation. These predators looted shops from Los Angeles to New York. Those minorities endanger human lives; they aggravate the destruction of the poorest neighborhoods.

Iconoclast protest

The antiracist protest that is spreading all over the world becomes iconoclastic, and the first to suffer are the statues of people. Until yesterday, they were considered beacons of civilization, but not of freedom and democracy. On social media abound the photos of the statue of **Columbus,** shot down in front of Capitol of Minneapolis. Unknown vandals beheaded a statue of the Italian explorer in Boston, Massachusetts. Police, who opened an investigation, found the decapitated head and "various pieces" on the ground. By now, there have been various attempts to remove or demolish statues or monuments considered symbols of slavery or colonial regimes, not only in the USA but also in Britain.

Another statue of Columbus had been torn apart and thrown into a lake in Richmond, Virginia. Protesters used various ropes to remove the icon, with an inscription that read 'Columbus represents genocide' planted on the base that supported the statue. In the United Kingdom, the anti-racist fury fell not only on slave trader and philanthropist **Edward Colston**, but also on **Churchill**. And in a country that until yesterday was an empire, there are many possible targets scattered in parks and gardens.

Colston had been a benefactor of the city. With the money he got from the slave trade, he had financed philanthropic works in nursing homes, schools, and churches. In the past, the statue had already been contested and also the object of a city petition to make it disappear. Once knocked down, a demonstrator took a photo on his knees on the bronze figure, mimicking the gesture of the white policeman who suffocated George Floyd in Minneapolis.

It was the same supporters of Black Lives Matter who compiled a list of 60 statues that they want to tear down because they "celebrate slavery and racism." The interactive map, *Topple the racists*,[4] was produced by the Stop Trump Coalition and lists plates and monuments in over 30 cities in the UK. On the list, there is the statue of **Robert Milligan**, the founder of the slave market, West India Docks, at the Museum of London. There is the statue in Edinburgh of former secretary **Henry Dundas**, who delayed the abolition of slavery, and there is the statue of Sir **Francis Drake** on the Plymouth Hoe.

Manchester City Council decided to anticipate the vandals and announced the 'revision' of all the statues in the city. In Plymouth, the authorities have decided to rename a square named after the slave trader **Sir John Hawkins**, although they have made it known that they do not intend to remove the statue of **Sir Francis Drake**. Among the growing protests, the

---

[4] https://www.toppletheracists.org/

Museum of London has decided to remove the giant bronze figure of a plantation and slave owner, **Robert Milligan**.

Also, in London, a demonstrator climbed onto the pedestal of The Cenotaph, the war memorial in Whitehall, and set fire to the flag with the Union Jack. And so the Mayor of London, Sadiq Khan, announced that a new commission would review the statues, monuments and street names to make sure they "reflect the diversity of the city."

The statue of former British soldier **Robert Baden-Powell**, who founded the Boy Scout youth movement in 1908, has also been temporarily removed from the British seaside town of Poole Quay to prevent it from being destroyed in protests. Accused of Nazi-Fascist sympathies, Baden-Powell had never hidden his views on homosexuals and racism. The president of the territorial council, the LibDem Vikki Slade, although "famous for the creation of the scouts," it must be acknowledged that "there are aspects of Robert Baden-Powell's life that are considered less worthy of commemoration."

In Belgium, the figure of the former king, **Leopold II**, is controversial for his colonial past. A statue dedicated to him has been removed from a square in Antwerp and will be kept in the storerooms of a local museum. A petition launched by a 14-year-old Belgian to ask for the removal of all the statues of the monarch, who inspired the bloody colonial regime in Congo from Brussels, has been signed in a few days by more than 44 thousand people and has also been accepted by the majority parties in Parliament. The government has been asked to set up a working group to "decolonize" the public spaces of the region: review and eliminate the names of streets and squares that contain references to the colonial history of the country, in particular King Leopold II (1835-1909).

More videos

After George Floyd's case, more videos showing African-American killings following a police check popped up.

Maurice Gordon

A video released by the New Jersey Public Prosecutor's Office dated May 23, 2020, two days before the events in Minneapolis, shows the killing of an unarmed young African-American. The images show Maurice Gordon, 28 years old from Poughkeepsie (New York) who is stopped by Sergeant Randall Wetzel for alleged speeding. The officer asks for details, like any routine check, and calls a tow truck because the car seems to have broken down. In the 30-minute video, you can see Wetzel asking the young man to sit in his waiting car. The policeman offers him a mask and a ride to a car dealership. After 20 minutes sitting in the police car, Gordon takes off his seatbelt and gets out of the vehicle. Wetzel yells at him several times as they seem to be fighting on the outside. The prosecutor's office reported that Gordon tried to get into the patrol seat twice and that the officer reacted first with the stinging spray and then pushed him out and shot him six times during a scuffle. The whole thing lasted less than a minute. The officer was suspended, pending the outcome of the investigation, after being stopped in New Jersey by a white cop for speeding.

Rayshard Brooks

27-year-old Rayshard Brooks died after being shot by an officer. The scene was filmed by several witnesses who later posted the social videos. Brooks was sleeping in his car in the parking lot of a well-known restaurant chain when police arrived on the scene. After testing positive for alcohol, Brooks resisted arrest by officers who used a taser. However, the 27-year-old managed to escape from the grab and was shot in the back by three gunshots fired by one of the two police officers while avoiding.

After the event, thousands of protesters invaded the streets of the city of Georgia to express their anger at the killing of the 27-year-old African-American. The protesters then gathered at the place where Brooks was killed and blocked the highway around the city. The restaurant outside where police shot the 27-year-old man was set on fire. Protesters shattered windowpanes and threw fireworks into the restaurant. At least 36 people were arrested.

CONCLUSION

The Minneapolis crime has revealed all the flaws in the system: in America, one citizen is arrested every three seconds. Almost 5 million Americans have been in prison, many of them for minor infractions. And African Americans go to jail at a rate five times higher than white people. There is no way to understand the last events of American history without seeing what happens on the other side of George Floyd's arrest and death in Minneapolis.

On one side of the story, four policemen arrest and handcuff a citizen on the word of shop assistants, who accuse him of paying for cigarettes with twenty counterfeit dollars.

On the other hand, there is the system of mass imprisonment, in which one can enter for even lesser offenses than a (presumed) fake banknote, which makes the United States the nation with the most inmates in the world.

There are 2.3 million people currently behind bars, scattered among over 7,000 states, federal and local prisons: a rate of 698 inmates per 100,000 inhabitants. According to data from Prison Policy[5], one of many projects is to reform the prison system, where half a million are awaiting trial. Often they don't have the money to wait for a verdict to free people because of bail costs, on average $10,000, or eight months' salary. The numbers of the

---

[5] https://www.prisonpolicy.org/reports/pie2020.html

problem become even more impressive if we look at citizens arrested by the police every year. According to the latest figures aggregated by the FBI[6], there are 10.3 million, a rate of 3.152.6 per 100,000 inhabitants.

We are talking about an entry into the penal system every three seconds, most of which will lead to no charges and no trial. The numbers have a very high scale: almost 5 million Americans have been in prison, and 77 million have a "criminal record." Nearly one in two (113 million) has a direct relative who has been in jail at some point in his life.

It is as if being arrested is now part of the American experience, especially for minorities and the poor. The specter of what is considered punishable in the United States is a fishing net launched every day over cities. Eighty percent of arrests nationwide are for an infraction at this level, an anecdote of which the local press is full: children arrested at school for being hyperactive, sheriffs organizing raids on teenagers accused of having a beer.

This approach leads to devastation in people's lives, and can lead to the loss of jobs, homes, scholarships, and custody of children. It can also undermine physical and mental health, and above all, creates a disproportionate number of dangerous and

---

[6] https://ucr.fbi.gov/crime-in-the-u.s/2018/crime-in-the-u.s.-2018/topic-pages/persons-arrested

unnecessary interactions between law enforcement agencies and citizens.

This system intertwines with racial discrimination, and it is here that the social mix becomes explosive. It is an essential key to understanding anger, after the events in Minneapolis.

The police murders are the fuse that detonates a wider unease because, for an African-American, the issue with the police and justice is a personal matter. African Americans are 13% of the population, but they represent about 40% of the prisoners. Black people in America are incarcerated at five times the rate of white people, and in five states (including George Floyd's Minnesota), at ten times the rate. There are twelve states where half of the prison population is made up of blacks. There are eleven where one in twenty adult African-American males is currently incarcerated (in Oklahoma one in fifteen).

Among the boys in the 2001 class, one in three will end up in handcuffs at some point in his life. Statistically, an African-American born after 1965 without a high school diploma is more likely to end up in jail than not. California and Michigan spend more money keeping young people in prison than educating them.

There is a correlation with suspensions and expulsions; school policies of zero tolerance bring black and Hispanic adolescents out of the education system, and into the penal system in later years. No one can argue that there is inequality in treatment. Still, the reasons have been debated for decades: education, unemployment, poverty, and the legacy of urban segregation end up in a cauldron that has not produced unequivocal answers. Wherever you look at it, the system has its own specific fault to repair, but these days it is the police forces that are most talked about.

In 2018, Johnnie Rush was on his way home to North Carolina after a 13-hour shift as a dishwasher. He was stopped by two policemen who accused him of not crossing the lines, even though it was night, and there were no cars. They handcuffed him, tasered him, and they were choking him. Also, he said, "I can't breathe." America is full of such stories: what strikes, even before the unjustified violence against an unarmed citizen, is the avoidability of the situation. One moment, there is a non-threatening person who is coming home, and minding his own business. The next minute, there is an arbitrary, violent, and dangerous fight, all for something for which a European would not even accept a fine. Rush was saved, when a video[7] was released, he was also cleared of all charges. The policeman lost his job and was indicted. George Floyd didn't do so well, unfortunately.

---

[7] https://www.washingtonpost.com/news/morning-mix/wp/2018/04/03/i-cant-breathe-asheville-police-video-shows-white-officer-beating-choking-black-jaywalking-suspect/

There is talk of reforming the police, improving their preparation, increasing bodycams, encouraging dialogue with communities, and being more productive with the violence. In Cary, North Carolina, police officers gathered to wash the feet of the leaders of the protest over George Floyd's death. It was a symbolic gesture of humility and a religious rite practiced by Christians along the lines of the foot washing that, as recounted in the Gospel, Jesus did to the apostles.

Derek Chauvin will probably have a long sentence. But nothing will change as long as America remains the country that arrests a citizen every three seconds.

***

This book remains with an open ending because we want to write the end once and for all. An end to prejudice, and to the fear of diversity. A diversity that does not impoverish a country, but enriches it.

We are looking forward to writing about the reforms that have been implemented. As in the past, there was the reform that abolished slavery; we hope that today there will be a reform that will not only reorganize the police in the country, but will also be aimed at closing the social gap, the real enemy and cancer of our society. Because we know that the real cause of all this is poverty, unemployment, early school leaving, and disrespect for minorities.

Lightning Source UK Ltd.
Milton Keynes UK
UKHW021307191120
373690UK00012B/990